394 Tu

The kiss : intimacies from
writers

THE KISS

ALSO BY BRIAN TURNER

My Life as a Foreign Country

Phantom Noise

Here, Bullet

AS EDITOR

The Strangest of Theatres:
Poets Writing Across Borders

THE KISS

Intimacies from Writers

Edited by BRIAN TURNER

W. W. NORTON & COMPANY

Independent Publishers Since 1923

New York   London

Names of certain individuals appearing in this book have been changed.

A portion of "Kiss, Kiss, Kiss" previously appeared in *Trophic Cascade*
by Camille T. Dungy and is used by permission of Wesleyan University Press.
"A Reckoning of Kisses," from *Heating & Cooling: 52 Micro-Memoirs*
by Beth Ann Fennelly. Copyright © 2017 by Beth Ann Fennelly.
Used by permission of W. W. Norton & Company, Inc.

For information about permission to reproduce selections from
this book, write to Permissions, W. W. Norton & Company, Inc.,
500 Fifth Avenue, New York, NY 10110

For information about special discounts for bulk purchases, please contact
W. W. Norton Special Sales at specialsales@wwnorton.com or 800-233-4830

Manufacturing by LSC Communications
Book design by JAMdesign
Production manager: Julia Druskin

Library of Congress Cataloging-in-Publication Data

Names: Turner, Brian, 1967– editor.
Title: The kiss : intimacies from writers / edited by Brian Turner.
Other titles: Kiss (W. W. Norton & Company)
Description: First edition. | New York : W. W. Norton & Company, [2018] |
Includes bibliographical references.
Identifiers: LCCN 2017056377 | ISBN 9780393635263 (hardcover)
Subjects: LCSH: Kissing. | Kissing in literature.
Classification: LCC GT2640 .K58 2018 | DDC 394—dc23
LC record available at https://lccn.loc.gov/2017056377

W. W. Norton & Company, Inc., 500 Fifth Avenue, New York, N.Y. 10110
www.wwnorton.com

W. W. Norton & Company Ltd., 15 Carlisle Street, London W1D 3BS

1 2 3 4 5 6 7 8 9 0

That night when you kissed me, I left a poem in your mouth.
You can hear some of the lines every time you breathe out.

—ANDREA GIBSON

CONTENTS

INTRODUCTION

Brian Turner

From Sioux Falls to Santiago to Paris, from Tehran to Khartoum to Reykjavík, Kyoto to Darwin; from the panchayat forests of India to the Giant's Causeway on the coast of Northern Ireland; in taxis and at bus stops and in kitchens and in sleigh beds and in haystacks and at airports around the globe people are kissing one another. This is not the scripted passion of Hollywood. The kissing that takes place in our lives is far more complicated and messy and human than the celluloid veneer of the silver screen. The kissing doesn't stop when the bombings take place in Aleppo, Madrid, Paris, or London. It doesn't stop when members of Pussy Riot are beaten and thrown in prison. It doesn't stop to consider Banksy's latest offering on the politics of art. It doesn't stop when Christo and Jeanne-Claude wrap the Reichstag in fabric and even when Christo says that it takes "greater courage to create things to be gone than to create things that will remain." The grandmother blowing kisses to her loved ones who are reduced to tiny images on an iPad, the eleven-foot-tall man leaning over to kiss the blaze of a horse's forehead, the distant fathers, the deported mothers, the generations of children—they are all filled with kisses as necessary as rain. And yet. The great and recorded moments of history mostly elide the profound moments, like *the kiss*, that comprise the very essence of our individual lives.

There are variations of the kiss that we need to explore and learn from. The ineffable kiss transported into language. The sublime kiss. The ambiguous kiss. The devastating kiss. The kiss we can't take back. The kiss we can never give. The broken kiss. The lost kiss. The kiss that changes a life.

One of the most memorable kisses I've ever witnessed took place at a Muay Thai fight during a ten-bout championship night at the Lump-inee Boxing Stadium in Bangkok, Thailand. The main event featured a young up-and-coming fighter facing off against the old champion. Tickets in hand, my wife and I sat ringside, eating sticky rice packed in bamboo containers and drinking Singha. A traditional musical trio— a hand drummer, a string player, and a wooden flutist—improvised music to match the intensity of the fight. The fight itself lived up to its billing as a pairing of two masters of the craft. And yet, what intrigued me most, stunned me, really, was what happened immediately after the young fighter kicked the old champion in the head, laying him out cold on the canvas. Initially, and predictably, the young fighter ran barefoot to his own corner, near us, and leapt up to stand on the first set of ropes, his gloved hands lifted upward in victory while a cheering of flashbulbs covered his body in light. At this moment, at the apex of his success, his knuckles and feet still stinging with the win, the young champion now crossed the ring to kneel before the old champion he'd just dethroned. The beaten man sat on a stool now, a cool towel draped over his head, aided by members of his team beside him. With the world looking on, the young champion bent over and kissed the tops of the other man's feet. An astonishing act of reverence. I've never seen anything else like it.

And yet. I typed the last paragraph while sitting on the eighth floor of a cancer ward while my wife received two whole units of hemoglobin, a dose of steroids given as a precautionary measure to reduce the swelling in her brain, and a series of other drugs. We heard a harp playing a few rooms down, and soon learned a wedding was under way. The bride was still in her twenties, and in my mind's eye I pictured the family gathered around the bed, a photographer in the back, everyone in their finest, some with tissues in their hands, the priest leading the ceremony. Such a fierce and soon-to-vanish thing—*love*. The bride's mother reaches over to gently moisten her daughter's lips with a cool swab, brushes her hair back from her forehead, and rearranges her daughter's opened veil. In Spanish, the priest says, "You may now kiss the bride," and the young man leans over to kiss his wife. And she doesn't close her eyes at first. She wants to see it all. To take everything in before the tears overwhelm her and, as weak as she is, to raise her arm and touch the side of his face as they kiss.

It's like this the world over. Some kiss a trophy and hoist it high over their heads. Some kiss the Blarney Stone. Some kiss the very ground at their feet.

As you read this, a teenager practices kissing a mirror, imagining that first-ever kiss with S_____ from fifth-period science class, her eyes open until the moment lips touch their own cool reflection, an inexact gesture toward transcendence, the violin rehearsing for its duet, testing the limits of the soul within the human frame, learning to shape the notes that rise over the music and then disappear.

A man in his seventies leans over the railing of a hospital bed to kiss his younger brother on the forehead—once the respirator has been switched off, the EKG flatlined into a digital silence—while those gathered around the bed have turned to hold one another, some of them sobbing, one of them considering how tender the kiss is and how the arc of two lives over decades of moments has condensed into this one sweet gesture, though the cooling body of the dead can offer no gesture in return.

A soldier, soon to return to war after a few days on leave, lies in bed with a woman whose last name he doesn't know, the word *muerto* tattooed on her inner thigh. He wants to wake her and also wants her to continue sleeping forever with her head on his chest, knowing that when she wakes she will kiss him and that it could be the last kiss of his life. And yet, when she wakes, he will kiss her as if it isn't the last one ever, as if it's just a kiss between brief lovers, a small hunger of the body and not a portion of the soul saying goodbye to a world near the end of its days.

There's a mother in the county jail, kissing her nine-year-old through the bulletproof glass in one of the visitor booths, the child angry and crying and sullen and saying, "I love you, too," as the bored deputy on duty pauses a moment to let them kiss a while longer like this before tapping the microphone and saying—as the mother motions with her hand as if smoothing the child's hair away from her eyes, the way she sometimes did early in the morning or when putting her child to bed—"Time's up. Time's up."

And the USS *Oak Hill* has docked in Virginia, with Petty Officer Second Class Marissa Gaeta getting the coveted "first kiss" on the dock with her girlfriend, Petty Officer Third Class Citlalic Snell. It's a kiss worthy of a postcard, a lean-back movie star kiss with two brunettes kissing until the world around them diminishes and sloughs away. This isn't a 1940s kiss. This is an eighty-days-at-sea kiss. This is the longed-for kiss, the I've-thought-of-this-moment-every-night-since-I-last-saw-you kiss. A kiss of solitude. A kiss of absence. Something made of starlight over a moonless ocean. A kiss to mark the sailor's return.

And there's a couple making love in a Mosul park, not far from the Tigris River, pausing to look each other in the eye for longer than they've ever done before, the sound of a pickup truck rolling not too far off through the eucalyptus grove, an explosion in the distance, as they continue to kiss now, though shifting somehow in response to the world and the cruel weight of time itself, to kiss soft and slow, kissing truly for the first time, a kiss that erases the kisses they've shared before, or maybe simply changes the nature of their kissing forever on from this point—now that they've slowed themselves long enough to really see one another, and as they imbue the word love with an altogether new layer of meaning.

For this anthology, I've invited writers and thinkers to share their thoughts on a specific kiss: an unexpected kiss, an unforgettable kiss, a kiss to circle back to. My intent here is to focus on kisses that—at least in some sense—attempt to bridge the gulf, to connect us to one another on a deeply human level, and, as closely as possible, to explore the altogether messy and complicated intimacies that exist in our actual lives, as well as in the complicated landscape of the imagination.

THE KISS

El mundo nace cuando dos se besan.

The world is born when two people kiss.

—OCTAVIO PAZ

THE LAST KISS

Nick Flynn

The Queen, asleep in the forest, her body laid out on a stone slab. Moonlight on her cheek, the blanket that covers her is blood-red. A willow weaves a mottled canopy of dark above her.

This, like many fairy tales, centers on a kiss.

If the Prince finds her in time he can wake her, but he is unsure which path to take—maybe the ravens have (once again) eaten all the bread-crumbs. If he gets there too late then she will never wake up.

The moral, if there is one, is that there really is no way to know when something—anything—that you do everyday, or even something you've done only once, will turn out to be the last time. The cup you drink your coffee from each morning—your favorite cup—is already broken. If you can think of the cup this way then you will, perhaps, hold onto it more tightly. Perhaps you will appreciate each moment you still have with it until it does, finally, forever, break.

Everything is already broken.

The kiss that comes to mind, if asked, is the last kiss I gave my mother—it rises up, unbidden. It's dusk, she's upstairs, lying in her bed, coming out of—or going into—another migraine. It's just after Thanksgiving, I've come home for a few days for the holiday. I'm living outside of the house by now, finishing up my junior year at college. My mother is still young—forty-two, still beautiful, still desired—young enough to start over. Her boyfriend's been in jail for a couple years now (he got caught smuggling drugs). He's up for parole in a month, but while he's been away she's been seeing someone else. I've been out with friends, likely getting high in our cars in the Peggotty Beach parking lot—these days I am always getting high. I'm home now to say goodbye, to let her know I'm about to get on my motorcycle and push on, ride back up to school. I climb the stairs to her bedroom. The lights are off, a tiny orange bottle of white pills within reach. Her eyes are closed, her blanket is red, her skin alabaster—maybe she's a little high herself, or a little hungover. The Queen is in pain, maybe mortal pain. If she doesn't open her eyes she might never open them, the Prince knows this, he's been wandering this forest his whole life, the breadcrumbs all eaten. The Prince leans over her face, as he had done so many times, to whisper the words that will keep her there, only the words don't come, or they come out wrong. *Can I get you anything?* The voice coming out of him (*see you soon*) doesn't even sound like him. *Kiss her*, it murmurs, & so he does & her eyes open & the spell, for that brief moment, is broken.

NOTES ON THE INVISIBLE KISS

Aimee Nezhukumatathil

Through wing, through vein and brittle wrist bone, how I kissed and moved with you still remain. After all this time you'd think I'd forget—already the sounds of a lost coin or click of a locket clasp I can't recall, the first notes of an ice-cream truck on your street: gone. There's a place in Lake Superior where butterflies veer sharply when they fly over a particular spot. No one could figure why such a change, such a quick turn at that specific place—until a geologist made the connection: a mountain once rose out of the water in that exact location thousands of years ago.

These butterflies and their butterfly offspring can still remember a mass they've never seen. Can remember sound waves breaking just *so* and fly out of the way. How did they pass on this knowledge of the invisible? Perhaps this message transmits in the song they sing themselves on their first wild night, spinning inside each chrysalis. Or from the music kissed down their backs as they cracked themselves open in the sun. Did milkweed whisper instructions to them as it scattered in the meadow?

And maybe that is the loneliest kind of memory: to be forever altered by an invisible kiss—something long gone and crumbled. Maybe that explains why, in the distant future, a gorgeous sound will still wound even my great-great-great-great-great-grandchild—a sound she can't quite place, can't quite name. That sound will prick at her and prick at her. And that sap-sticky pine needle will be a chalky kiss smudging her hands with a pale color found only in the crepuscular hour of the day.

An invisible kiss is like that: what you remember won't come from a single script or scene, but from, say, the surprise of purple quartz inside a geode. The first time I smashed one, I put it inside a sock so any shards wouldn't slice into the dark iris of my eye. And after the first careful taps, I clobbered it, already trying to prepare myself for disappointment: a sock full of crumble. But when I slid out the pieces into my palm, I couldn't believe my luck—the violet-rich sparkle!—and suddenly I was back in ninth-grade science class and timed quizzes to identify minerals on the Moh's scale of hardness.

Everyone knew talc was the softest on the scale and everyone of course knew diamond. Hardly anyone remembered the minerals in between. But I was always drawn to quartz—I lingered over it the longest, flipped it over in my hand, even tasted it when no one was looking: like campfire smoke left in a shirt.

Once, when I vacationed in the Keys, I scattered my pastel treasures from the beach—coquina shells—on a windowsill before bedtime. I did not know they were still alive. When I woke, the tiny clams had sighed open, their tongues evaporated during the night. Who knows how many invisible kisses covered me while I slept?

THE KISS AT DAWN

Pico Iyer

steal out of my little room with the first call to prayer, and take a taxi
through the darkness to the central souk. The stores are shuttered
now, but the thronged smell of spices and bodies is everywhere,
overwhelming. I walk past the great mosque, a center of the Islamic
world since the eighth century, and along the thin alleyways that fork
this way and that through the Old City of Damascus. Then, as every
morning, I arrive at the marble floor that leads to the golden shrine.

A little door admits me to a space as brightly lit as a nightclub, where
a young man, black-suited and rosy-cheeked, is singing of the love that's
recently deserted him. Bodies are everywhere, hunched over, shoulders
sagging, faces turned up now and then so I can see the tears glistening,
running down their cheeks.

At the center of the space an old man is kissing, kissing a bejeweled
grille as if saying goodbye to the woman he'd loved for sixty years and
now will never see again.

I watch him, rapt, as pieces of colored glass in the windows send exploding reflections all around, and see him turn away, red-eyed and shaking. An old woman now is kissing around the same area, and she might be kissing the son she's sending off to war.

A slim, elegant young man is running his hands over the golden sepulcher protecting the body of the great-granddaughter of the Prophet, dead for more than a thousand years, and then he runs his hands over his face as if to transfer the magic. Stooped figures are walking up to the glowing box that encases the shroud and kissing it, kissing it, as if to pour their hearts into this long-vanished girl of four.

For forty-one years now, I've been traveling the world, in large part to see people give themselves over to what they adore. The black-hatted men pressing into the corners of the Western Wall to confide their secrets—their prayers—to the ancient stones, the pilgrims carrying toy cars and bathtubs over the mountains to a shaman priest outside a cathedral in Bolivia. The white-robed figures walking for weeks to the cut-rock churches of Lalibela, the faces reflected, gleaming, in the flickering candles of the Jokhang Temple.

But never have I seen a sensual intensity and beauty to rival what I've found in Islam. Taxi drivers in Isfahan recite the verses of Rumi, hymning a love that leaves him senseless and intoxicated; their cousins in Syria, eyes closed, breath heaving, cluster before first light at the graves of long-dead saints, bereft; even the roughest men in Damascus allow their hearts to break and bring their lips to a grille in homage and supplication. If you want to see what true love is, go—even if, as in my case, you're a Hindu from the U.S.—to the Shiite mosques in Sunni Syria and watch in silence.

A kiss, you see, can carry not just a heart in it, but a soul.

INTERLUDE

Kim Addonizio

For some reason, young, sometimes young and drunk, strangers are drawn to me. That night I was at a club in New York with my brother Gary, listening to jazz. I stepped outside with a hitter of pot he'd handed me. I sheltered from the rain under a small overhang and lit up, then stood a few minutes longer, watching the lit needles of rain dissolving into Sixth Avenue. A twenty-something blond boy veered over. He was Norwegian, he said, and visiting the city alone. He was adorable and also, clearly, wasted. I was several decades older, but there was no mistaking the fact that he was flirting with me.

"So, what are you doing the rest of the night?" he asked.

"I have to go back inside to my boyfriend," I lied. I had no boyfriend. I was wondering if I'd ever have one again. When you are a woman over sixty, even one who looks, if I may say so, pretty damned good, the boyfriends are scarce. How long had it been since I'd kissed a man? Let's just call it a while. As for the rest of what might naturally follow a kiss between two lonely people—let's call it a long while. I have several women friends near my age who are counting it in years; one has a decade under her belt. So to speak. "My life is over," she wailed recently. This is an exceedingly smart, talented, witty, lovely woman. She makes me desperately wish we were both gay. Unfortunately for us, we are drawn to people with penises.

And here was one swaying before me, ready for a night on the town. I could have taken him home and had my way with him, but what did I really want? Let's call it more than an inebriated fuck. Let's go ahead and call it love, real love, the kind I'd experienced more than once in my life, and missed now.

So here I was, pleasantly stoned, about to blow off this guy instead of blow him, or worse.

Then I had an impulse.

I took his face in my hands and kissed him on his pillowy Norwegian lips. They were cold, and tasted like beer and rain. He closed his eyes in delight. I closed mine, too, our bodies a few inches apart, the faint sounds of the band mixing with passing voices and tires on wet asphalt.

How long did it last? Less than a minute. A few of his molecules waltzed into my mouth; a few of mine whirled into his. Then I turned and ran back inside.

Later, I thought about Chekhov's mournful Officer Ryabovich in "The Kiss," who remembers his "little adventure" with a stranger in a dark room. First he thinks the kiss will change his life; then he concludes it was trivial, and is confirmed in his own sense of inadequacy. Finally the world seems "an unintelligible, aimless jest."

The world often strikes me the same way. But I prefer to find the joke funny. And to believe, in the weird and sometimes happy accidents that result—in this case—in kissing a beautiful stranger in the rain. It didn't really change anything, but it wasn't trivial. It was one of those encounters that rises up out of nowhere and sinks back into it, giving off light and energy as it goes. It reminded me that my life isn't over. That we can't know what's next. Let's call that a reason to be happy, alone, enjoying a night out with a brother you love, listening to musicians improvise over the changes.

THE KISS I WOULD HAVE SPENT ON YOU

Laure-Anne Bosselaar and Kurt Brown

finally had the courage to turn on Kurt's computer in September. He had passed away in June, and Steve Huff, the editor and publisher of Tiger Bark Press, had asked me to find Kurt's poetry files, in order to publish his posthumous collection, *I've Come This Far to Say Hello: Poems Selected and New*. A mellow sun filled his room, the curtains open as he always left them—the small bronze abstract sculpture we had bought at an artists' market in Provence next to the pile of books, Jim Shepard's *You Think That's Bad*, Edmund Wilson's *Axel's Castle*, Charles Simic's *My Noiseless Entourage*, and a bilingual edition of François Villon's *The Legacy & the Testament*, by his reading chair.

As I sat at his desk, a graying woman stared back at me from the black mirror of Kurt's computer monitor, her left hand clasped against her lips at the thought of opening his files. I turned the computer on and, though filled with hesitation, soon discovered a file called "Almost

Poems," which was comprised of about eighty to ninety poems, all in alphabetical order—some in very early stages of draft, some unfinished, others almost done. I read through them avidly, one poem after another. Hundreds of lines I had never seen:

I'm thinking of your eyes, following each word now / as I write this, / as I place words end-to-end with other words to build a bridge, a sentence / over nothing. / We both are children once again, / stepping out into a field of snow . . .

I can hear Kurt's voice when I read these words. And I'm transported by this field of snow to the years we lived in Snowmass Village, Colorado, sometimes cut off from the main roads by snowstorms and whiteouts that lasted for days, and for which we were secretly thankful.

There is a place in which beauty will not die, / timeless Eden where memory lies down / with desire and age is only a dream. / Where flesh is immortal, and willing, and warm.

Kurt and I loved listening to music together. I remember often listening to the Romanian Women's Choir, or to *Chants D'Auvergne* by Canteloube. We'd sit, not saying much, sipping wine, and, yes, for an instant, feeling ageless, and willing, and warm.

The body is but a visible portion of the soul, like thoughts, whose surrogates are words. / And when thoughts dry up, words are dust / whipping across imagination's grave.

Then I opened "The Kiss."

Read it, reread it, read it again.

I don't quite remember how fast or blurry-eyed my drive was to Arroyo Burro Beach, about five minutes from our house. But I do remember standing knee-deep in the ocean, as close as I could be to the black, split rock next to which I had dispersed most of Kurt's ashes. It was high tide—I couldn't quite reach "his" rock. And I remember I very quietly wept there, elated, brokenhearted, thankful, and full of sorrow.

THE KISS
for Laure-Anne

That kiss I failed to give you.
How can you forgive me?
The kiss I would have spent on you is still
there, within me. It will probably die there.
But it will be the last of me to die.

BAZOOKA SMACKDOWN

Patricia Smith

There were two ways up and down Schurz High School. The front stairs were lit insanely, huge banks of fluorescence unleashed to bathe scurrying students in a blinding blue. I took the creaky and shadowed back stairs when I tired of being the school's official colored girl, when I wanted to get in a little weep between classes, when I was late again for algebra and its confounding reams of hokum.

The back stairs, also unofficially known as "Make-Out Row," was where young love—in all its overwrought, conjectural glory—went to messily implode. In the shadows were hitched and squirming bodies, rushed and fevered hands. There was much smacking and slurp, the moist sound track of curiosity's little engine.

But the knowledge of all that fluid being exchanged didn't register in any carnal way. I was fifteen, scrawny, and bumbling. The dozen black students, in a class of eight hundred, were publicly derided as love (or lust) interests—we walked those halls like little raised fists, portents of the world outside pushing to get in. It was 1970. We were enthralling and terrifying.

One Tuesday, when Make-Out Row was eerily unoccupied, I was rushing down while Dan Mikros (his name has been changed to protect the dull-witted) rushed up. Dan Mikros with the exactly two errant mud-brown hairs popping from the jut in his chin. Dan Mikros, that chin peppered with whiteheads (haha) and scarlet blotch. Dan Mikros, linebacker, thick head, thick neck, thick chest, and all the stupid that suggests. Dan Mikros, usually huddled outside a bank of lockers with other Bulldogs, making a snarl face and hissing the *n*-word whenever hive mind mustered the guts. Dan Mikros, who suddenly saw his chance to covertly integrate the Row, striking a blow for civil rights while answering the question his fidgety dreams couldn't stop asking.

My head was down, as usual. (All through high school, I was not a fan of eyes.) I moved to pass him, and a thick hand, nails bitten to blood, pressed resolutely against my chest. I lost my balance, stumbling backward into one of the Row's prized crevices, and then his open mouth was on my face. That boy damned well knew the clock was ticking. So he made me know that frenzied mouth—the morning's Bazooka, flecks of tobacco, a vague eggish stench, and spit, sluggish like an oil across my tongue. His ham hand pumped my budding left breast like it was trying to extract information from a mute prisoner.

I knew this knee-jerk tryst was the biggest risk of Dan Mikros's muscle-headed little life, and when his bedeviled thing went *kapow!* behind his zipper, I was all the reason. I shoved him, hawked admirably, and watched my spittle drip from a stunned blue eye and cascade through a pimpled landscape of cheek and chin. I hissed, hefted my little fist, and mused for a second about the consequences of bringing it down.

Then I brought it down.

THE SUMMONS

Mark Doty

Suppose you made a taxonomy of kisses, in their vast variety: the kiss on the cheek of a child heading out for the day, the kiss on the forehead you give a friend departing after she's unburdened herself in a long conversation, the complex vocabulary of kisses between the long-coupled, who signal through them a host things. But those aren't the kisses you really want to study.

Could you name the kisses of lovers, distinguishing their nuances, the shades of passion? You would like to do the research for this. But then you realize it's what you have been doing, what you are doing, what you plan to do.

A catalogue of kisses, each one documented by a sentence, a sketch, or a photograph. It could be digitized, like Emily Dickinson's herbarium in the exhibit at the Morgan Library; touch the stems or leaves you like on the screen and a new window shows you Latin and common names, uses, culture, references to the plant in her poetry. But in the great album of kisses, the master text, there would have to be so much room! The sorts of kisses which are invitations, their degree of fervor indicating greater urgency or intensity. The lips-shut small kiss you give to the shut lips of a man heading out your door in the morning when you don't plan to see him more than just this once, and you know he's already made the same decision. The different sort of closed-lip small kiss you give him when it's his apartment you're leaving. Is there room, in the imaginarium, for the kisses you've withheld? Because they wouldn't have been welcomed? Or you were afraid they *would* be welcome, and promised too much, and then you'd somehow have to make room for that? Or the kiss withheld because you knew someone wanted it, and you weren't about to give him that?

When _____ used to kiss me I felt he was hitting my mouth, striking at me with the teeth beneath his lips. Why didn't I stop him?

My mother's kiss, when it came, seemed to carry with it a small disturbance of air which carried her scents: a floral soap from Mexico, lipstick, coffee, a bracing whiff of alcohol from the neck of a just-opened bottle of vodka.

❧ ❧ ❧

The first time I kissed _____ we were standing on a fire escape, at night, behind an old hotel, and there were freight cars moving on the tracks beneath us, tracks that spread in all directions into the snow.

❧ ❧ ❧

You're just warming up to the one kiss you really want to talk about.

❧ ❧ ❧

When that kiss comes, it doesn't matter that you've known him for a few years, in an easy way: lightweight, sexy, and pleasant, something breezy about it, as if he blew in now and then on a wind arrived from a climate where gravity doesn't work as hard as it seems to in New York. He's always seemed young, not attached to anything much, though perhaps that's because he just hasn't told you much. You always like him, his freshness and his enthusiasm for pleasure, which is why you keep seeing him again, though the expectation's just for a few bright hours.

And then, as we say, out of the blue, out of nowhere, without anything obvious changing, something shifts, imperceptibly but clearly, like the atmosphere after a storm: magnetic charge, ions, something in the clockworks. There's a newly opened space, an aperture in which the kiss can take place. You're lying together, face-to-face and half undressed, you've done this many times, but the unexpected way your torsos fall into each other, unwilled, is the overture, and as your faces come together the kiss, before it's a kiss, is a fuse that begins a long burn, a nearly visible black sparkle traversing more of a distance than you'd imagine, coiling its way through the space between you in two directions, into his chest as well as into yours. Hello, light and heat, hello, next-ness, and then

his beauty laid out like an entire field of candles in yellow grass. You saw it before but never saw it, not all lit like this. Hello.

His beauty an explosion inside a clear room at the bottom of the ocean, the shock wave just now reaching you,

beauty the defining character of his body, but not resident there only, connected instead to something larger, above him, free-floating cloud, suddenly ours in common, and from there spilling down into me, until I'm lit up also, a cove of small waves crested by phosphorus.

The kiss is immense, although you understand at once—not a thought exactly, more a felt understanding—that its intimacy is what allows for this tremendous scale. Does the kiss even have an edge? It goes on, in every way; why would you want it to stop, except to take stock a second, to catch your breath so you can dive into that wave again?

And go under, and dive again.

It takes a while to know that the space in which you live, the element in which your body moves, has changed. From here on out? With each immersion, you are less contained. To be that desired, what is that? To have that opening, that entrance awaiting you, to know it's there. To dissolve the edges of you, that it isn't just the mouth, just the body, that is opened by the kiss.

From the first moment you know that the kiss is a fact, as real as this table and chair, both utter promise and total trouble. If *this* is in the world, this possibility, if you know the address of such a place, where the flaming meadow and the light-edged wavelets dwell in the late hours together, where his beauty is the solvent in which you both are dissolved and remade in the crazy furnace of the kiss, why would you want to be anywhere else? It's an imperative, a summons, a bell. And what are you going to do about that?

THE SECRET KISS

Ilyse Kusnetz

This is a kiss that happens in secret. A smoky kiss. I press into it—sometimes a desperate fumbling, at other times calculating and deliberate. Each time, I wonder what it says about me. But then I look in the mirror at the wreckage left to me: the wild, thinning hair; the swollen face; the body misshapen by so many treatments and drugs—radiation, chemo, steroids, drugs to aid memory, drugs for nausea, drugs for pain, drugs for the side effects the other drugs bring.

Sometimes it's an ache, a violent cramping in my stomach that drives me to press my lips around the smooth glass and kiss. Lately it's my bones, as if I'm trying to fill the space inside them, sharp and crumbling. The tumors on the PET scan look like radioactive snowballs tucked into vertebrae and ribs, liver and lungs. I close my eyes and see them glowing.

Sometimes this kiss is the only relief I can find, and I believe in its healing power. And yet, self-recrimination is never far away. It's still a forbidden lip-lock, and with each inhalation that takes me closer to letting go, part of me wonders if I've become like one of Odysseus's lotus eaters, or if this is somehow just a fast track toward drowning in the River Lethe. Is it okay to check out, I ask the air—to kiss my pain away with such verdant fervor? Such kisses once sparked passion and signified defiance, but this trembling need is something else entirely.

In the Netherlands recreational marijuana is frowned upon by the general populace, but there's no stigma attached if you have a medical condition. It's recognized as medicine. You're not a pothead if you're genuinely sick. But I want to defend my kiss even further: I wish a good death to the Puritan inside of me who believes suffering clarifies the soul. I push away my doubts.

With each inhalation, my reflection relaxes—like a cat circling and kneading a nest before settling down, sighing, content.

Imagine pain as tendrils of smoke, exhaled, piping up in one white, faded corner of the room, coalescing around a light-saving bulb. The fan is always on, buzzing the wispy gray contrails into oblivion. Beautiful and ethereal.

My lover is patient. He understands the smoke is also a signal, a nod to the universe that something beyond my control possesses my body, my psyche. I am part shaman when I lift the colorful pipe; I am part dying woman when I take its heat into my lungs.

Every breath resurrects me. Every kiss brings a kind of grace.

WHERE SCARS RESIDE

Major Jackson

1

January, ten kilometers southwest of Oaxaca City, smack-dab in the
middle of the Monte Albán—where the Zapotecs over the course of a
thousand years flattened a mountain to build a city. You are here for
a week to lead a poetry workshop, but first you and the other partic-
ipants survey these epically old temples, tombs, and ceremonial plat-
forms accessed predominantly by way of extreme ascents up steep
pyramidal steps. The sun stings your eyes even with shades. And here,
in the center of the Great Plaza, squinting, you gaze upon a couple
in their early thirties kissing for five minutes or more, one of those
breathless, deep-in-it kisses, one of those the-world-swirls-around-us-
and-we-might-as-well-be-its-sole-inhabitants kisses. They are fashion-
ably dressed, maybe too done up for the climb, the ancient red and
beige dirt coating everyone's shoes and feet: he in slacks and a sky-blue

short-sleeve and she in a cream silk blouse and burgundy print wrap-around skirt. Their intimacy so dissonant, you look around in search of a film crew: a script supervisor, a director, a costume designer. Both wear straw hats, which she holds to her head whenever a gust of wind occasionally sweeps across their bodies as though buffeting them. Just when the edges of their bodies begin to blur in the rippling heat, they pause and take each other in, their eyes dissolving. Cut.

2

Filmmaker Ingmar Bergman once reported in an interview: I have maintained open channels to my childhood. Sometimes in the night, when I am on the limit between sleeping and being awake, I can just go through a door into my childhood and everything is as it was . . . the sudden aggressivity of the adult world, the terror of the unknown, and the fear from the tension between my father and mother.

3

Daily you walk into your childhood of violence, like a sequence in a film seen too many times that becomes your dream. Except this was your home, among potted plants and a vitrine cabinet of rare china: the dull smack of your drunk grandfather, who raised you like his when your teen parents could not, hitting your grandmother, and she fighting back with all the might her Jesus could muster those whiskey-heavy nights. Then, the only other sound: their tortured breathing and her cowering, balling up like a loose fist to fend his last blows; their bodies indistinguishable. You took it in, especially Friday evenings when late arrival from work and one of the local speakeasys was guaranteed, and it became your air, choking you, too, on the exhale until the next morning, finally awakening to the bright rustle of the kitchen to find them at a red Formica table laughing, she kissing the top of his head as she slid behind him, simultaneously reaching for burnt toast, everything is as it was.

4

Their remoteness stretches over ancient pebbles, a mystical isolation by their own directing, an open-air music of touch that announces more love than desire, all underscored by a deluge of sunlight which feels Mediterranean in mood. No one bothers them. For the most part, no one takes a second notice, despite the passing minutes of uninterrupted, slow head swirl and lip press. It's a Monday. Only two other small groups are here; the vastness of the land makes it seem you are few in number. Speaking in various languages, visitors saunter by; others cast sideways glances, never too distasteful, just enough to gather unto themselves this sacred act on sacred ground, among the shadows banyan trees make and leaning slabs of stone portraying castrated men, in the presence of the dead waiting out once more this invasion of the living, wishing they, too, could once again press themselves into the shape of a beloved, wishing they, too, could maintain channels.

5

One Saturday afternoon, you watch a late-teenage boy, slightly older than you, in a white ribbed tank top, along with his four sisters and mother, move boxes out of a beat-up Chrysler into the three-story row home at the corner of your street, vacant for several years. You never learn their names. Your friend Curt sits across the street and catcalls to one of the girls, the one with the slick ponytail down her back. After getting his designer sneakers snatched off his feet last spring, he has been lifting weights, bulking up into a walking wall of human meat.

"Girl, you fine as daylight. Come over here. I want to be your sky." Despite her smiles and giggles, her older brother, ignoring how flattered she is, warns him to back off. "Or what?" says Curt. "Imma kick your . . . !" This goes on for half an hour, the brother unloading floor lamps, hangers, prepackaged food, a laundry basket full of cleaning supplies while defending his sister's honor from sexual taunts until Curt says finally and offhandedly, "Let's go," meaning let's get it on.

6

Your grandfather is trembling as he loads the chambers of his .357 Magnum, which he has just retrieved from his army-issued footlocker. Your grandmother is in front of him, pleading with him not to go out. His only surviving sister Margaret just called to say her husband James beat her up again, pretty badly. "Cille!" your grandfather says. "I'm just going over there to scare him. Dammit, woman, get out of my way!"

7

How do they do this? Both make their way to the center of the street, with Curt taking off his shirt careful not to break his trot, speeding up slightly such that when he arrives his right fist, firm and close to his shoulders, unloads into, less a punch into the man's left jaw and side of his face, but more a meeting of his perspiring body with that of the other man's, who crumples unconscious on the asphalt, a clash erotic and intoxicating as a kiss as much as it is frighteningly repulsive. He stands above his victim quietly, heavily breathing, his brute face scanning the streets and neighbors who have assembled around him. All of your life, you think of that one fluid motion of power, terrorized by the fact we are capable of such collisions, such harm, such leveling of each other to flattened mountains, left to tunnel into ourselves,

such wretched unhappiness, such unfathomable cruelty unless resur-
rected by the tenderness and affection of a lover, by kisses that leave us
enthroned.

8

Such gentleness of touch when they breathe together. Like always in
the presence of couples seeming to take plunges into a beloved's body,
you are stuck, unable to turn away. Their kiss heals all around them. It
is like Stevens's jar in Tennessee: it takes dominion everywhere.

9

In Bergman's film *Scenes from a Marriage*, Marianne tells Johan: "Sometimes it grieves me that I have never loved anyone. I don't think I have
ever been loved either. It really distresses me."
　　Sometimes we go through doors.

10

In this land far from home, you squint and stare at a young couple kissing. Their love reaches somewhere deep inside you that needs healing,
where scars reside. You convince yourself they want an audience; they
need onlookers to bear witness, to receive and complete the endowment of the love between them. You can sense their chests beating, see
from here their eyes opening and closing in wonder. You are less awed
by these ancient temples where Zapotec priests performed human sacrifice. You are awed by a man and woman kissing countering the trau-
matic violence in our lives, the emptiness, all the blood and grieving
spilled over the Earth.

A SYMPHONY IN RAIN

Kazim Ali

Here now under the accumulating pile of ash from when the cathedrals lay down and rain wrote itself across the sky.

Drawn across the strings, how can you sing blue thread into pools spooling.

Ghost lover rejoin me. Sense me and send me rejoin me.

Danger the thundering chords that bind you.

Mouth meeting a mouth, in the cold, outside. In a public place, a street corner perhaps.

And desperate because there is no time. You have an appointment, he has a train to catch.

Drenched in the ink from the letters, soaked in it, spattered across chest and neck, pooling in the hollow of the clavicle.

Disappearance of words, each one a black bird written against the storm-gray sky.

Cathedral of rain unspooling blue from the sky. Mark me with rain. Spill all the words.

Pieced through or pierced.

A letter written on the page in white ink, confessing everything, declaring everything.

More likely a thousand letters, each written on top of the other on the skin of my chest and stomach, the small brush licking me, licking me.

Rain rushing down the steps of rue des Eaux for the river. A bronze statue of John the Bapstist, rain and river mixing around his feet.

Who am I. Who I once was or who I wanted to be.

Every day I ask for signs every day I fail to see.

Rubbed the inkstone with the wet brush. Light wash of ink. Crisp letters. Spell out the story of your last desire in every space. Choruses of light and languor.

Soft feathery touch on my skin, ink brush or tongue, sand drizzled over. Ash.

How do you linger, what do you hear. The low box in the resonant harp.

Blue and gray and white reaching down in strings and rivulets, wet upon you.

Wet upon you wonder, a picture drawn slick in lines.

Shorn after the storm, streets wet with asters and deletions. Rain still ringing in your ears.

Charmed by the sky's seduction.

His tongue in my mouth, wind on my body or water. Warm in the moment after the storm.

Rain drying on the paving stones. Rain-soaked leaves in drifts along the streets.

Haven't you seen my palm where it's written the twenty-seven stars, lines crossing each other.

Even as he pulls away to run for his train, I fling the thought after him: I want you to press yourself against me, write this minute into my skin.

From rue des Eaux to the Trocadéro Gardens I run as the sky begins again its overture.

It is a failure. I am soaked. I slow down to walk.

On the bridge, under his improvised awning, in the half-rain, among the umbrella hawkers and scattered sunbeams, a portrait painter sits, waiting.

Will I sit? he asks me, the rain already intensifying its demand, streaking down my face, my neck, into my shirt, along my chest, my wet stomach, down below my waist.

And if there is ash and rain mixed with ink how will you draw a face or body, quivering in time, a day drenched a person become another.

Write the rain, I beg him. Write it on me with your mouth.

KISS, KISS, KISS

Camille T. Dungy

1. GOLDEN AGE

I was closer in age to the baby than to the me I am now. On an island. Summer. There were eight of us. We had nothing to do. I don't remember sleeping. We had so much to do. We took turns reading *The Hobbit* to each other. What would it be like to live in some other, almost ours, world?

We ate fresh fish and veggies, drank lots of beer. Some of us kissed. We only took care of each other. We only took care of ourselves.

We swam through the days, argued just a little. Some others kissed.

Nothing of the way we were resembled life now. Nothing about me has changed.

One afternoon, I got up from my towel and started walking. *Where are you going?* asked a friend.

Toward the horizon, I told her.

That friend would come to my wedding. Would come to my baby shower. *Should I tell the others you'll be gone awhile?* she asked.

Yes, I told her. *Tell the others I'll be gone awhile.*

2. THE TICKET

I'd thought this would be a reflective time, but parenting is a now-centered endeavor. I may have to think about tomorrow, but then again, I have to think about assuring tomorrow will happen *right now*. Yesterday is over. Yesterday things happened that impact us *now*. This part of my life is running in the present tense.

I can hardly remember her birth, let alone the first time I kissed her.

Her birth, the first time I had a chance to kiss her, these are stories I tell like my other stories, urgently, but fuzzy on the details. Like the story I tell about the convenience store worker. On his last day in that bleak store, he bought a lottery ticket and won—was it a thousand dollars? Let's say he only won a hundred. He reinvested his winnings into—was it a hundred tickets? Twenty? That's not the point, see. The point is that *now* he's a millionaire.

3. LAST KISS

Mom called today. Just to hear my voice.

She spent the morning ushering at a funeral. A thousand people: every seat in the sanctuary, chairs in the narthex, the fellowship hall. People lined up from seven in the morning.

A seventeen-year-old—volleyball star, newspaper editor—riding home from youth group.

Her organs, eyes, ligaments, and skin were rushed elsewhere in lifecopters.

One mother—her daughter completed suicide three years before—

told the other volunteers she came to acknowledge how they'd helped her. *I know I never thanked you. Every time I went to write a card*, she said, *I couldn't.*

My friend Sebastian was in an accident last week. His heart is bruised. What happens when your heart is bruised?

Caterpillars live in the passionflower bush over my girl's day care. When I kissed her goodbye this morning, five butterflies circled my head.

LIGHT YEARS

Rebecca Makkai

Some of the many things I don't remember from that winter, my senior year of college: the moment I realized how late I was, or whether I told anyone else, or why I didn't consider buying a test or at least going to the infirmary. What I remember is finding the boy inside the entrance to the English building and, because we were alone, telling him. It was a day or two before Christmas break. We'd given each other sweaters, and he was wearing his.

I remember that I took every opportunity to hop down steps, to flop stomach-first on couches. I was dizzy, nauseated, terrified.

In retrospect, there were alternate explanations for my body's shutdown. At five-foot-seven, I weighed 115 pounds. I'd had a fever, on and off, for eight weeks. I was in such bad shape that although I passed all my English classes and even my last-ditch-science-requirement astronomy course, there are huge swaths of senior year I can't remember at all. I'll re-watch movies I know I saw that winter, and nothing. Books I read for senior seminars: nothing.

I recently learned from my daughter that when Cassiopeia was cast into the sky as a chain of stars, an angry Poseidon ensured she'd spend half the night standing on her head. I must have learned this in 1999, as well. I'd have appreciated the story.

I do not particularly remember what the boy said, just that one of us was headed to class, that it was a brief exchange, comforting. I assume we recited the standard script. ("How late?" "I'm trying not to think about it." "Everything's going to be fine.") What I do remember, sharply, is the sad, sweet, reassuring kiss that ended the conversation. It was not romantic or sexual or platonic. It was not a parting kiss or a questioning kiss or really like any kiss I'd particularly known to exist. It was a kiss on the lips, but it might as easily have been a kiss on the forehead.

It was a time machine to a point in my life where kissing would not be an imitation of a movie scene or a simple demonstration of desire—a point where it would always be in some ways about the fraught past, the fraught future, and yet, in that same moment, a refuge from those things.

There are first kisses, and then there are first kisses. This wasn't the boy I'd spend my life with, but it was the first kiss of the rest of my life.

I was not pregnant. By June, the boy and I had broken up and reconciled and then broken up again for good. I had memorized, for my astronomy final, every constellation in the northern hemisphere. Names and shapes and myths I'd forget by July.

When I look up now, I'm back to just Orion and the dippers. The other stories—virgins frozen in flight, venomous snakes, grieving mothers—are a blur.

But isn't it good to remember they're there? To know my life was briefly enriched by their gorgeous, complicated names?

KISSING JOE F_____

Philip Metres

Burly Joe F_____ had a mouth that never stopped. I'd never played basketball against someone who talked so much. Throughout the game, he talked to himself, to his teammates, to his opponents. Most of all, he unleashed a nonstop flood of invective toward the referees.

My college intramural team was a hodgepodge of athletes and gym rats, the Black Student Union president and vice president, alongside some of the whitest guys you'd ever meet: Sweet Lew and Cookah, Philson and Ferrera. Everybody could ball, and we were poised to upset Joe's football-jock squad and head to the championship. We were leading by a few points, but Joe—an all-conference offensive lineman, the son of an African-American professional baseball player—tried to haul his team back by words alone.

The ref whistled a foul. Joe rushed into another one-sided debate with the ref, his tank-like frame leaned over the cowed freshman. Joe's index finger menaced the air between them.

Not knowing what I was doing, tired of Joe's verbal attack, I approached him, placed my lips on his salty-wet cheek, and kissed.

Stunned silent, Joe turned to face me.

In college, sometimes I felt like I was playing my own punk version of Gandhi, heading off violence with softness. It's true, I was a peacenik. I organized a rally against the Gulf War, served at a soup kitchen, and helped to found the Peace and Conflict Studies Program. I wrote poems, which a buddy joked meant that I "cried a lot."

But something in me seethed. I lusted tongue-tied after girls, utterly and unrequitedly. I couldn't write a good poem, and was envy-green of my creative writing classmates who did. I regarded the varsity jocks with a mixture of jealousy and judgment. So on the hoop court against them, my angst would turn me briefly into an olive-skinned Hulk, slashing toward the basket, hurtling and hurling myself against all my outer and inner limits. Aching to prove myself. To be a man.

Dear reader, I wish I could say I let the kiss do the talking, my sweet and salty subversion.

I didn't.

"That's for acting like a woman," I said.

To cut this man down, I betrayed all women.

Joe chuckled, tongue-stuck. He wiped his sweat-sheened forehead, jogged back to play defense, and didn't talk the rest of the game.

I'd forgotten about that episode until now, a lifetime later, as my wife and I watch my thirteen-year-old daughter lope down the basketball court. From the oceanic vaults of my memory, among all the other kisses of my life, this one floated up—like a corpse.

I'm ashamed I couldn't let that kiss burn like a strange wet star on Joe's cheek. I had to erase its mystery with macho misogyny, with locker room sexism.

If only I kept my lips pursed shut, perhaps my act of disruptive brother-love could have sunk down, deep down, all the way down— into the kisser and the kissed.

HALF FABLE

Terrance Hayes

The giant many fans know as "Mega Tall Paul" was approximately half a century old the first time his father kissed him. Giants are difficult to kiss unless one is also a giant. As you know, Tall Paul towered in a realm of his own. The current *Guinness World Records* lists him as a clean eleven feet tall. He is in fact eleven feet two and seven-eighths inches. After Tall Paul told the cashier who asked his height the other day he was eleven feet two and seven-eighths inches, she said with a frown, "Why you gotta add the *seven-eighths*, ain't eleven feet two already tall enough?" Tall Paul wanted to kiss her because no one else in all his years had ever told him it was a vain thing to say. He was well known for his large self-regard, but told the cashier he was only trying to sound exact. He wanted to kiss her for her illuminated critique, and if he had, it would have required severe bending. Mostly Tall Paul hugged people to his waist, he did not bend. Most of the fans who lined up to greet him after his shows were children. Mostly all he did was stand around. He poked his hands through the holes cut in the top of the circus tent when he raised his arms—a show highlight. Occasionally he wanted to kiss one of the lovely indifferent mothers of the children who were his fans. Sometimes he wanted to be kissed by one strange woman after another. He missed his wife. He was a passionate man. His shirt pits always had a kind of sweat and sugar smell to them. Occasionally he wanted one of the grown-up women to breathe his scent. Mostly all he did was stand around. His wife was not especially impressed. His mother, brother, and father were definitely his biggest fans. Tall Paul was glad he'd get to spend a couple of days with them in Florida. He wanted them to see how well he was doing. His extra-long shoes and clothes were tailor-made, he had been on the cover of a few little-read magazines devoted to freak fans. He was a minor celebrity, but at eleven-foot-two-and-seven-eighths inches tall no one needed to know who he was to gawk at his height. Three different security agents pulled him aside to take selfies at the airport when he landed. Sometimes he searched for images of himself posted on Instagram. Usually the picture was of some stranger wildly grinning beside his crotch. A few times it was just a shot of his nostrils and the bottom of his chin. When Tall Paul hugged people to his waist, it was not unlike the way his father and brother, two average-sized black men, hugged people. His father and brother were military men. His father and brother were sports fans. His father and brother did not kiss one another upon greeting. Tall Paul had just about freaked out when a foreigner at one of his events decided, upon realizing he could not kiss Tall Paul on the cheek, to kiss the giant's large narrow hand. Any kiss in the region of his waist, which was just about all kisses when they happened, made Tall Paul blush. One of the security guards, a fit Hispanic woman, taking a selfie with him at the airport, kissed his hand. He got a slight erection. He thought of the woman's hair and mouth and breasts and ass along the entire cab ride to the home of his brother in Tampa. His brother, an average-sized man, jumped from military aircrafts for a living. The giant liked to think it was because it gave his brother a view of his life. The giant suspected his brother was lonely falling from those heights. His brother's daughters met him at the door when he stooped, practically bowing as he entered the house. The daughters, giggling, seven and ten, hugged Tall Paul's kneecaps. He pulled two coins made of pure three-hundred-year-old silver from his pocket and passed one to each of them. He nodded toward the mother of the girls, his brother's wife, his sister-in-law. He wasn't sure what she thought of him. Tall Paul went down to his knee and kissed his mother. She had been waiting to kiss him. He had flown several hours from a land of twelve-month snows into a land of twenty-four-hour humidity. She would never tell him if he smelled unpleasant. He kissed her on her jaw; she kissed him on the cheek. Then, as the giant's father half hugged him, the giant accidentally, almost automatically, kissed his father on the cheek. It was a peck, really, distributed closer to his ear than his cheek, burning imperceptibly as they pulled apart. A blush of silence opened, for a moment, between them. Even if the giant had not been a giant, he would have known, as all average boys know, boys do not kiss men; men do not kiss. The summer Tall Paul was sixteen, for example, before his father left for Korea, his father told him he'd be the big man of the house and shook his hand. When his father returned a year later, he shook Tall Paul's bigger, longer hand in the same way, perhaps a little firmer. Rarely has the giant kissed standing perfectly upright. When the time came to kiss his petite bride twenty years ago, he fell to a knee, lifted the veil, and leaned into the soft clearing between her ear and shoulder blade, kissed her neck. He did not kiss his father the day of the marriage despite the wide smile they shared. In Florida when the giant's father embraced him, he could not ever recall a time they'd been that close. Without thinking he kissed the side of his father's face. The kiss was so near his ear, the giant could have whispered something about sadness to him. They pretended it had not happened.

But that is not the story I intended to tell. I intended to tell you about the first time my father kissed me. He probably kissed me when I was a boy, but I'm fairly sure he hadn't kissed me since I was seven or eight years old. I was taught as all boys are taught: boys should not be kissed; men do not kiss. The thing I feared most happened: I became a middle-aged cliché. Consumed by the ways my parents damaged me. Insecure, reckless, lonely, a strange voice echoing in a giant helmet. I'd taken a plane to my brother's home in Tampa so the four of us could drive the two hundred or so miles to Miami to see the Dolphins, my father's favorite NFL team, play the Giants, my brother's favorite team. During the drive my mother asked why I wasn't wearing my wedding ring. Whatever I told her, she accepted for the time being. Or she was thinking, *I can't believe you kissed your father.* Everyone fell silent when it happened. My father didn't quite look me in the face. My brother slapped his hands and said something about the football game. My father wore his Dolphins jersey, my brother his Giants cap. My mother and I were dressed like civilians at the game. It occurred to me the men wore face masks perhaps to avoid kissing. The Giants won by two touchdowns. My brother teased my father, poking him in the ribs before patting him on the back. Just as we began climbing the stadium stairs, a cussing ruckus broke out between two drunk white men sev-

eral rows below. A tattooed muscular man swung almost gleefully in
the direction of a smaller man who ducked and dodged swinging in
retreat. After a few hot moments they quit as if realizing we bystand-
ers would not intervene. My mother reprimanded the security guard
who'd watched like the rest of us as the two men flailed failing to land
a single blow. We had two separate rooms at a hotel across from the
airport. I'd have to catch a plane out of Miami early the next morning.
My mother brought over two small cups of some kind of peach-flavored
schnapps, glancing once more at my bare ring finger before exiting. My
brother and I stayed up late talking. The next morning, before heading
to the airport—I meant to wait until the last minute—my brother and
I went to our parents' hotel room. I'd had a dream the night before.
The four of us were seated in the stadium. From behind me I could
hear someone saying, "Don't you come nowhere near my grave! Don't
you come nowhere near my grave." That's pretty much all that happened. The men we'd seen fighting at the end of game did not appear
in the dream. The stands sloped into oblivion. They were full of stadium trash, but they were empty. I didn't tell anyone about it. I almost
mentioned it when my mother shook her head mumbling something
about premonition the next morning. They had slept separately in the
room's double beds. For some reason my mother had made her bed.
Flowers were printed on her new pajamas. Her hair was immaculate. I
have never seen her tend to her hair, but I have never seen a hair out of
place. When I kissed her on the top of her forehead, she smiled just as
her granddaughters had when I kissed them the day before. My father
sat on the bed with tears on his face. I had seen him weep at his mother's funeral; I had heard him crying on the other side of a door that year
he and my mother came close to divorce; but I had never seen him sob

the way he did that morning when I told him my marriage was ending. I can't describe it, the gentleness. It shocked us: my brother, mother, and me. No one said anything. Then he rose and embraced me for what felt like two or three minutes. My face was against his shoulder. Before letting go, he kissed me, quickly, softly.

THE EVOLUTION OF A KISS

Nickole Brown

Let it begin. Not at the beginning, but with ants, maybe, unacknowledged makers of this world they are, opening capillaries in the soil so it might breathe. Let it begin with ants, a highway of them in and out of their busy kingdom, the tickle of their hinged antennae in greeting, a chemical exchange, then a kind of flirtation—the beckoning of mandibles, a barely audible tap-tap-tap not unlike pebbles thrown up at the midnight window of a beautiful girl. We want to say everything begins with us, that creatures feel the way we do, so scientists will tell us not to be fooled into thinking this is a kiss. But watch as one nestmate joins another at its mouth—from one to the other flows sustenance, a body-warmed surplus of sweetness.

Then let's skip ahead, a step up, past the lizards, up into the air, to birds. The crop milk of pigeons and flamingos, how their throats swell for their young, their tongues dripping a necessary curd into waiting, hungry mouths. Or all those nest hatchlings with beaks brightly

5

marked on the inside that, opened wide, make for a mother's beak a bright directive, a diamond-shaped landing pad. Then there is something closer to what we know of a kiss—courtship feeding, all those cardinals and kingfishers passing treats between them as maybe you did at the back of the school bus, an exchange of chewed gum in lieu of a for-real smooch. We cannot call these avian offerings a kiss, not exactly, but still, Darwin knew something we hesitate to admit. When he wrote, "They fell in love with one another," it was no remark about a Victorian courtship—he was talking about a pair of ducks.

Obscenely rushed, but you know what's next: the mammal tongue, warm with its own blood, decked with a surface to taste and scour the one place another animal cannot reach on its own body—its head and face. There is logic here, how each furred being can only groom itself with the lay of its own hair, but groomed by another, the cleanse is deeper, dislodging what needs to be removed, a taste that digs against the grain. Here, too, is the fox lapping the face of his mate, the nipping of hyenas and nuzzling of rats, the puckering chimps, the male elephant in musth—his face inviting taste, literally seeping with desire.

So let us not make a kiss into an abstraction, a metaphor planted on your own palm and blown into the air. Because everything human has its animal beginnings. The kiss—born of an empire of tongue and spit, of hunger and itch—is a break in the dam separating two beings that agree, *Yes, please touch me there*. An insane gesture, at least on paper, to open our most necessary and vulnerable aperture and surrender it to another, to give over that place with which we eat and speak and breathe.

For me, this long song leads to East Eleventh Street, New York. Nine years ago now, maybe ten. Leaning in her doorway, the taste of her mouth stained with the aftertaste of pomegranate tea. It was the first time I was close enough to see how shallow the divot at the base of her neck, to smell something of the city's traffic in her hair. I didn't know I'd found my wife yet and would not know for years what I had found, but my mouth knew. My tongue knew. And the creatures before me, they knew, too. The whole aching chorus of them, all the way back to single-celled beasts who swallowed each other whole not to eat but to make what was two into one. That first night, that evening in December, our first kiss was already wired deep within. I am no scientist, but still, I try to count the ages that made that risk; I count and bless the thirty-four muscles of my human face that made that kiss.

KISSING MELISSA

Benjamin Busch

Before I ever kissed anyone, I was kissing Melissa. Fifth grade, and it was sorcery, a figment of fire, a girl in my head. It happened without language, a wave closing in, wild and necessary like mating. There isn't a cure for this new awareness when you're young and drunk with it. Gravity always makes you fall. It wore me down, those long days passing in the halls, glimpsing her on bleachers, and sitting close in class. I would gaze and get caught, but she didn't know how passionately we were already involved . . . and I didn't know how to tell her. I wanted to sleep so I could kiss her again.

Dances in the school cafeteria were the only times to see her in a transcendental state. Lights low for slow songs gave us all brief courage, like animals in evenings when the sky is small with darkness, when the world is a place you can hide in, and I would pace the edges, overcome, afraid of the chance to hold her for a few nervous moments.

Just asking for a dance burned all my bravery. We stood straight and separate, my arms stiff and hands hot as we circled, turning like a universe, a sun between us. She smiled and I couldn't say what I'd rehearsed. All the songs spoke for me. All the songs replied. All the songs were about her.

And so I kissed her thousands of times while we slept, kept apart by hills and fields, rivers and nights. It was like a premonition, the touch of our lips, an urge I can't articulate, even now, our heads tilted and eyes closed, a waking dream, an exchange of vows. These were fantasies— so I was good at kissing, the two of us standing, fit together like a braid. It felt urgent and hallucinogenic, our bodies blending. She bewildered me with a sense of certainty, a red flush of longing. She gave me a fever that lasted a decade.

I tried to look away. Entire relationships swelled and fell. Sweet kisses happened with others while this perfect one lay coiled within me. I wondered how she would taste. I wanted to change my face, the way I walked. I wanted to be other boys, better boys, grow differently, defy ancestry and biology. I started acting on stage, but I couldn't be anyone else enough. I wanted to press my mouth to hers, feel her voice on my tongue, pull the breath from her lungs, the heat and wet of her love drawn in like steam, one hand in her dark hair, the other on the small of her back.

This may be your story, too. We drowned, you and I, electric with yearning and its desperate indignities. High school arced until it ended, all of us suddenly blown into the rest of our lives, these loves moored where we dreamt them. We can't summon that first flame with the same feral immediacy, that chemical burn in our blood, but those days are there, stored somewhere like damp gunpowder. I've never forgotten her. It was a beautiful romance and lit my way to immensities. Melissa comes back to me sometimes, a flicker, thirty years later, but she's still a girl, her face blurred by layers of memory, someone else now, someone else then. I finally know what I'd say if I were still a boy. It took never kissing her to find the words.

KISS, KISS

Ira Sukrungruang

I

My six-month-old son knows the sound, the electric trilling that comes from the tablet I hold in front of him. When he hears it, he giggles, smiles, and waits. What will emerge, he knows, is an old woman eight thousand miles away, in a country where purple lotuses bloom in ditches, a country currently without a government. To my son, this woman is magic. She appears suddenly from a dark screen, and what he sees is not her face but the top of her forehead and the dome of her black hair. He grabs for the woman, believing she is there in his Florida home. The woman says hello in two languages—Thai and English. She says his Thai name, Po, over and over again. This old woman does not know that we can hear her perfectly; she does not need to shout. This doesn't matter to my son. The old woman's forehead is familiar. Her voice. He loves the sound of his name spoken in a foreign tongue.

II

The hours before he arrived, the sky was cloudless, the day bright. But a storm gathered quickly and thrashed against the hospital windows. The lights outside lit the rain speckles on the glass into tiny globes of orange. This is what I remember from the outside world, those globes of orange light. Inside the room, the midwife could not find my son's heartbeat. My wife knotted her hands in the sheets and howled. I put my head against hers, whispering clichéd encouragement. *You can do this. You're doing great.* But I wasn't sure if she could do this. I wasn't sure whether she was doing great. The clipped voices of the midwife and nurses seemed to suggest otherwise.

The midwife said it was time. Said, This boy wants out. "I can't hear the heartbeat," she said.

"You need to push."

And my wife did. Through tears. Through screams.

"I got him," the midwife said. "He's arrived."

The silence that followed. A silence among the chaos of nurses and orderlies. A silence between my wife's heavy pants of breath, my reverberating heart.

Then the sound of his first cry.

After I clipped his umbilical cord, after the chaos of the night subsided and my wife was resting in her bed, I watched my son—my son!—breathe in a bassinet beside the bed. I kept watching, in fear that I might lose him. I put my lips on his wrinkled forehead, and like my mother, when she kissed me good night those many years ago, I breathed him in.

III

My son does not give kisses. He devours. He will take your face in both hands and open his mouth wide and seek to encapsulate the whole of you. He will take your nose, your forehead, your chin. His kisses are a possession.

Except for me.

He does not kiss me, though I spend the majority of the day with him. Though he reaches for me and cries when I leave a room. He loves me, I know, but he does not kiss me. My wife says it's because I don't have boobs. My mother says I need to get rid of my scratchy beard.

IV

The old woman wants to see every element of my son's day. She wants to witness his eating habits. How he sleeps. Bath time. She wants to see him jump in his jumper. Wants to inspect the state of his diapers. The old woman is too old to travel, her legs unable to withstand the twenty-two hours on a plane. So in the time we have she wants to observe her grandson's life. She says, I love you. She says how badly she wants to hold him. She says she wishes she had more time to know him. She says, Do you think he loves me?

At the end of every conversation, she puckers her lips and brings the screen in and out. *"Jube, jube,"* she says. Kiss, kiss.

And my boy opens his mouth wide, taking her whole.

TRIGGER

Lacy M. Johnson

want to say it begins with the boy in the baseball cap, one hand plunged deep into the pocket of his jeans; the other holding out a bottle, offering a drink. His cheeks glow red, lit by the booze and the midnight air. It is February and we are standing in an empty parking lot beside the highway. He offers the bottle again, says, *It'll keep you warm*, his breath making a cloud around his face. Where have I told my parents I will be? I am only fourteen, and he is a few years older than me. Tall, *like a man*, I think. What do I know? He is on the basketball team, over six feet tall. His mustache and chest hair appear in earnest patches. He takes a drag of his cigarette, blows the smoke over one shoulder. He doesn't take his eyes off me. What does he see? I lift the bottle to my lips, tip it back, and drink.

In the morning, my thighs are purpled with bruises from his sharp pelvic bones, a rust-colored stain on the sheet beneath me. My arm is sore at the shoulder, my lips swollen, full, and smashed-looking in the mirror. I bend over the toilet while the night returns to me in heaves and waves: our lips meet once, and then again, and then he is clawing and desperate. I want to move away from his kiss, from what is approaching and unstoppable, and let a "No" fall from my mouth— then a string of them dripping like pearls. Afterward he dresses and slips out the door. The bile in my stomach surges, acid and cinnamon and sweet.

I am only fourteen, and I do not yet know there is a word for this. I know the word—spoken as a warning, as a threat, a premonitory curse—but it conjures only the image of a woman crying out, a man emerging from the shadows to pin her arms and spread her legs. Maybe there's a detective fishing for a notebook, a policeman with a pair of handcuffs, a mother cursing the man and blaming herself. The word does not conjure a kiss that tastes like smoke and cinnamon and mentholated lip balm, so instead I call him my boyfriend, though it isn't because he walks me home after school, or because he calls after my parents go to bed. A girl in my homeroom hears what has happened and she explains the word back to me: "Slut," she calls me. "Liar. Whore."

I believe her, and so does the boy on the bottom bunk of his college dorm room, the boy on the golf course, the boy who corners me at the dance club, the boy at the party, the boy in the back of the car, the man who forgot a condom, the man on the motorcycle with tattoos for eyebrows, the man who tried to kill me, the man I married and then divorced. Their wet mouths form a chorus of unstoppable kisses.

I want to say it begins with the boy, that first boy, who kissed and kept on kissing until my body was not my own. How I got it back is another story. But as for him, I heard that boy never stopped kissing, not even when he put the barrel of a shotgun in his mouth, pursed his lips, and pulled the trigger.

A LETTER TO MY WIFE ON HER 40TH BIRTHDAY

Brian Castner

September 2016

My love,

Today you turned forty years old. Today my friend's wife died. My friend's name is also Brian. He and I were soldiers, we fought in the war and that meant we were supposed to die first. But he didn't die first, and now I see I might not, either, so I cling to you like you never had a shadow until today.

To celebrate your birthday we went for a hike. There is a hill near our home that is covered with statues. They call it a sculpture park: fantastical animals, nude maidens bathing, wrought-iron turrets and castles, enormous insects, a maze without a minotaur, and the busts of generations of women, all the way down the line. We walked the grassy paths among the sculpture, under a blue sky so sharp as to cut, and I held your hand and you knew I thought of my friend Brian.

That's why you asked me to write you this letter.

I never met Ilyse, Brian's wife. She died today, but she had been dying for some time. Brian and Ilyse are poets, and the more cancer she got the more poems she wrote, and that's why I feel like I know her a little bit, too. We had heard the end was coming. A ghastly relief.

Brian and I fought in an overseas war. We fought them over there so we didn't have to fight them back here, that's what everyone said. A year of bombs in a faraway desert was the cost of keeping you safe back home. I paid my lot, and gladly. But what war can I fight now to spare you even a sweet slip-off while asleep at home in bed? Of the two of us, I'm the one who hates to see you grow old. Not for the smiles around your eyes or sparkles in your hair, but because it exposes the lie that I can protect you indefinitely.

We stood in the bright meadow and looked across the hollow, untouched yet by autumn color. I smelled your sun-warm hair and touched your neck with my finger and laid my brow on your shoulder until your shirt was wet. I didn't say anything and you said, "We're very lucky."

If I could loosen my grip even a moment, I might hear those words. We were married so young. Everyone said we were just kids, and though I didn't believe them at the time, they were right. I grew up with you. Only half our lives together thus far, but you float at the edges of my childhood memories as well. I'm surprised, when I look at old school photos, to see you absent. I missed you before I met you.

But today, on your birthday, you're here. You are happy and healthy and sexy and strong. You have lived on this planet for forty years and I am somehow alive with you. Astounding.

How to spend your only fortieth birthday? Fearing and fighting what will pass, or cherishing that unlikely moment? I didn't speak this question aloud, but you answered, and in the most surprising and wonderful way.

You took off all your clothes and ran in the sunshine, and in that moment, all shadows were burned away.

That's when I kissed you.

Forever, Brian

FALLING

Andre Dubus III

t was after midnight, and we were standing on the flat tar roof of the Marriott Marquis in Times Square, fifty-six stories above the street. The light cast from below was the color of embers. We were so high just a few other buildings rose above us, and we couldn't hear the taxicabs moving through the square below, but from the short knee wall we could see them, small as dried kidney beans, though she had only glanced down for a second before pulling back.

Her hair was long, brown, and curly. She wore gold earrings, and it was late spring and chilly so she must have been wearing a jacket. She was twenty-six, and I was twenty-eight, and twelve hours earlier in Massachusetts she'd sat next to me in the backseat of my friend's car, and now we had known each other for less than one day. We'd been walking through the Lower East Side looking for a place to dance, but we got lost and ended up in a dark neighborhood, empty crack vials crunching under our feet. She had to stop to bend down and adjust the strap on one of her shoes, and she reached out her hand to me and I took it, telling myself I shouldn't, but I did anyway.

We continued walking. I kept her hand in mine, and we held hands all the way to Times Square and its unapologetic assault of neon where she needed to find a bathroom, and so we found ourselves in the grand lobby of the Marriott Marquis, where I waited for her, staring at the glass elevators sitting in the center of the carpeted lobby. Then she came out of the bathroom and looked so beautiful, walking with the straight-backed poise of the dancer she was, and I took her hand again and said, "Let's go *up*."

The elevator rose fast, and we could look out and see each floor of the hotel fall away beneath us. She stepped closer to me, close enough I could smell her hair, and that did something to me, and when I stepped out onto the carpet of the fifty-sixth floor I took her hand again, and said, "Let's go to the *roof*."

What I did not know is that she was afraid of heights, and what she did not know is that for months I had been trying to get over a longtime girlfriend by seeing more than one woman at the same time, trying to feel something substantial for each and failing, and so just a day earlier I'd cut it off with all three of them. I vowed to spend the next year alone, and so why was I holding the hand of this woman less than one day after leaving the others? Why was I pulling her up to the unlocked rooftop of the Marriott Marquis in Times Square?

Because hours earlier, sitting in the backseat of my friend's car, she told me that all she wanted to do was what she was already doing, which was to dance and to draw, and I wanted to look away from her dark eyes looking directly into mine, but I could not, for I had known this woman before, maybe many times, before my births and after my deaths, and now I wanted her to feel how high we were; I wanted her to see those tiny taxicabs of New York City. I could feel the knee wall pressing against my shins. I could feel the lighted city far below, faint car horns rising up like wisps of smoke.

She stepped back quickly. A small voice inside me said, *You're supposed to be alone now. It's time for you to be alone.* But when I turned away from the roof's low wall, she hugged me, and I could feel how afraid she'd been of falling, and then we were drawing closer and then we were kissing. It was soft and warm and lasted longer than I knew it should, for this wasn't my plan at all, it just was not. But I kissed her again, and I kissed her last night and this morning, too, twenty-eight years fallen away behind us, our three children grown and living elsewhere now, doing their own falling, one ride and climb and fateful kiss at a time.

THE RIDE

Siobhan Fallon

A city at night, seen from inside a taxi, can seem like any city, street signs and neon lights, the stop and go of city blocks, the skyscrapers and mini-marts. New York, Beijing, Tokyo, Honolulu, Dubai.

You devised this taxi ride. You wanted to be alone with him. You wanted this fleeting envelope of time, caught between two destinations, anonymous and dark, all those people outside the windows caught in the same human crush but oblivious of anything you might do.

The radio sings in another language, a stranger drives without speaking, all of it dares you, this last chance before you arrive at the train station, before you say goodbye. The two of you had sat next to each other on a couch at a party, your feet near but not touching. You got ready to leave when he checked his watch, assuming he wanted you to go with him. In the taxi, he put his seat belt on and you smiled, thought he was silly, what grown man wears a seat belt in the back-seat of a taxi? But you did as he did, playfully, wanting him to see your raised eyebrow, your side smile, to see you were game. And why else would he wear a seat belt except to create a barrier between you, an attempt to behave, to show you he felt like he must restrain himself?

That thought is all you need. You unclick your seat belt and move close. He tilts his chin at the sound.

"Just let me kiss you." You say this, you, and you are surprised at your predatory powers and territorial lean, you are small but in this taxi you are almost the same height as this tall and broad-shouldered man, and all those things that are female and weak are suddenly an advantage, that you can continue to move without waiting for more than his quick and helpless nod, the sigh that escapes him as if this is not entirely consensual, this is a capitulation, but that thought will come to you later—in the moment you are already pouncing, you are only thinking of your need to press and enter that contained male space of suit and tie, buttoned-up and armored in layers compared to the flimsy material so free and smooth on you. Though the distance is divided it is not so hard to cross, and the taxi is hurtling so fast now, so little time, how can you not try for it, this one small thing?

He is soft as a child, as an adolescent, as that very first game of spin the bottle in the woods behind a badly built fort. Twelve years old and discovering this strange game, Catholic school kids playing their own Pentecost, this new gift of tongues. Curious children testing the edges of sin.

His lips, his tongue, his cheek beneath your palm, smoother than you could have imagined.

There are countries in that kiss, years of experience, ghosts of past lovers and the tricks they taught you. Your lives peel off and exist on their own, future selves in all of their possibilities and computations, couplings and separations. It could be the beginning of everything. You can see it. You can see him and you want him there, in all your tomorrows. Anything can happen while you are inside that small, wet place, you believe in *forever* in a way you would never be foolish enough to believe otherwise, there's neither reason nor reality to ruin the soft click of teeth, the perfect alignment of lip and tongue, that necessary balance of suffocation and breath.

You would pay dearly to unclick a belt and so eagerly unleash yourself onto other things, other moments, other passions, to be so intent upon keeping a small flame alight that you don't care about anything else. But this, too, is something you will only think later.

The taxi stops. Grand Central Station.

Immediately you are two separate bodies. Immediately you are forced to be aware. You are embarrassed, finding yourself in his lap.

And you realize you have to pay, as you do in all things. You slide quickly back to your seat, reaching for the purse kicked over, your wallet on the floor, so clumsy. The taxi driver flicks on a light, perhaps to be helpful, perhaps to be an asshole, you must be red-faced, suddenly sober and shy now that you are no longer in motion, now that the cars outside are merely traffic, the streets dirty and strange. Your fingers search for the right bills, your mind trying to figure out how much you need to tip, but he tells you he will pay the fare, of course, because he will not exit with you, he will take this ride farther without you, to his own destination ahead. You can barely look at him, though you feel him watching, and your downcast eyes notice his seat belt is still buckled, that silver glint at his hip, that strap across his chest. How is it you didn't notice there had only been one attempt at release?

The realization catapults you out the door, everything that had seemed graceful suddenly awkward, your high heels, your legs, your very hands oddly loose at your wrists. There are pedestrians in your way, the streets too alive and loud and close.

You hesitate, wonder whether you ought to face the taxi and say your goodbye through the open window, or walk toward the station and hope he will change his mind and follow.

How could you have shared breath and suddenly be afraid that a glance will be too telling, too intimate?

But when you turn, you see you are too late, the cab is already driving away, the breath you shared was only air, the taxi windows opaque, nothing but the bright lights of a blind city reflected back at you.

HOLLYWOOD, ENDING.

Schafer John c

1: CHASING IT

I was an actor. After a rough upbringing and theater work in Chicago I was told I could possibly make a living at it.

I moved to Los Angeles. Two years later I found myself in the Hollywood Hills attending a birthday party for my well-regarded manager and two of her clients. One would go on to star in a long-running television show and subsequent films. The other would pinch my ass.

The party was an indoor/outdoor affair; crowded and I knew no one. As the most recent client signed, people did not gravitate to me. I ate, drank, and stood on the brick patio staring in awe at the thousands of lights dotting the surrounding hills. The hills themselves rose up against the night sky backlit by the ambient glow from the Valley on one side and the effulgence of Hollywood on the other. For a flatlander it was all hypnotic: the low music, the cool dry night backed by the pulse of a hundred people mixing in a limited space.

Inside and searching for the manager to say my goodbye, I turned sideways through the crowd, holding my drink aloft, and I felt the unmistakable pinch on my backside. I pivoted, more curious than annoyed, and she was there holding a slightly inebriated smile. We locked eyes. She was beautiful. It was L.A.. The room was beautiful. She leaned in. At five-foot-nine and wearing cowboy boots, she didn't have to rise on her toes.

"You looked like you were leaving."

"I was."

"You should stay and help us clean up." Eyes holding, her smile relaxed. Time bent. People rubbed by. Finally I responded:

"Now, that's an invitation." The corners of her mouth turned back up. I stayed.

Three hours later, on a deck above a ravine, we stood at her door. Hollywood shimmered below to our right, the hills all around, downtown L.A. a faint luminescence in the distance. A car hundreds of feet below wound its way small and silent up Laurel Canyon. The walk was easy and light, the neighborhood quiet, the alcohol burning off. The talk had been free and slightly urgent as if to catch up with the looks we had exchanged. The last ten minutes we had held hands. It was seamless and natural.

The door had a faint yellow bulb above casting an aureate glow onto the deck, and she turned to unlock, her hands betrayed the slightest tremor. Then she turned back to me, looked up, and we closed the foot of space between us. A mix of pent-up anticipation, raw sexuality, and need met. We used our lips, mouths, and tongues to reassure each other where we wanted this to go. I don't know how long it lasted. Finally we separated, hearts banging; her head on my chest, muttering, "Oh, god." We caught breath.

I remember driving home out of the hills toward the ocean thinking, *So that's what it's supposed to feel like.* I was thirty years old.

Almost five years later, after living together for four and postponing two wedding dates, she married someone else.

I had gone through a marriage and a live-in in my twenties. I was not dispensed toward believing pop locutions such as Soul Mate or Love of My Life. As if you could sum up the heart with a two- or four-word catchphrase. Well, you don't believe something, till you do. I eventually did.

That kiss.

I've chased it with everyone since, but never replicated it.

Now past fifty, I shake my head at the memory. Although it's been over two decades, sometimes up in the middle of the night, staring through the cast of moonlight out my back door, I think, *Perfect.*

2: KISS OF THE SPIDER AUDITION

After a few years in Los Angeles I found myself stuck in early morning rush hour. I was not happy. The obligatory traffic jam was not the only reason for my foul mood. I was en route to my sixth callback for what I had deemed "The Spider Movie"; a low-budget film centered around spiders mutated by nuclear waste that take over a small town. My part was the male lead, a sheriff, who is not only tasked with saving the town from glowing arachnids, but also falls in love with a beautiful nuclear biologist . . . who just happens to be passing through.

It was shit. But my agent said I had to start somewhere, and it beat throwing drunks out of a West L.A. bar five nights a week, which was how I augmented my career in the arts. It was four weeks of work at union scale, which was four months' rent.

What vexed me was the sixth callback, which meant they were seeing me for the seventh time. The third time through I had read for the director, a craggy-faced man in his sixties with a wispy goatee and a scarf the size of a horse blanket. After the fourth callback I thought we were done; union rules stipulated that you were compensated for any subsequent calls, and it was low-budget. Wrong. I got the seventy-five bucks for my fifth visit and all nine present got a healthy dose of edgy sarcasm before I read: "If you all call me back again we'll be spending Thanksgiving together and sending Christmas cards and shit."

I pulled into the parking lot deep in North Hollywood and cut the engine. I took a breath and let it out slowly. I reminded myself I was being paid to show up and it would surely be the last time because I was going to read with the lead actress. She was the little sister of a major movie star. Maybe talent ran in the family.

Inside the paneled waiting room the casting director took me aside. We were almost old friends by now, and in hushed tones she gave me the lowdown: "The scene you're doing ends in a kiss. Under no circumstances are you to kiss her. No matter what. Just embrace." I shrugged, said, "No problem," and took a seat. Four other actors sat around nervously looking at their pages. I got up to use the john.

The bathroom had a urinal and a commode separated by a partition. As I unzipped I heard the unmistakable sound of someone retching. I rose and peeked over, and sure enough a short muscular man was heaving into the bowl. As I finished my business he appeared at the sink next to me. He washed his mouth out and then fixed his hair. *He definitely shouldn't kiss her*, I thought.

I was the last called in. I counted eleven people in the room as I was introduced to the starlet. She was red-haired, blue-eyed, thin, and looked nothing like her big sis. We read the scene. The end came and I moved to embrace and she planted her plump lips on mine, her tongue entering my mouth like a lizard on a mission. The rule in the thespian profession concerning kissing is you don't use your tongue—it is considered rude and, after a warning, a firing offense. So as she mopped my teeth and the roof of my mouth, I froze. My own tongue cowered behind my lower gums. Time seemed to elongate. When she finally unlocked her mouth from mine, someone said softly, "Scene." I stood paralyzed at the breach in etiquette. As she looked at me with bright eyes and mussed lips I had to remember to close my sarcastic trap, which was sprung open like it had a bad hinge. Finally I stepped to the door, opened it, and heard her say in a breathy timbre, "I like him."

I did not get that job. I did not spend Thanksgiving with them. I did not save a town from spiders. But under no circumstances did I kiss her.

3: KISSING L.A. GOODBYE

I had left L.A. but I hadn't said goodbye. So I drove three hundred miles on four hours of sleep to try. The Inglewood cemetery is a flat expanse with all the headstones flush to the earth. The Great Western Forum sits across Manchester Avenue, its enormous circular structure vacant and surrounded by acres of asphalt. Planes roar low overhead en route to landing at LAX. The flight path had been a hot topic decades earlier, but the poor lost out and the dead didn't care.

I came to Los Angeles fourteen years before to try and make a living in the movie business. I worked on the margins of that industry: enough acting gigs and writing jobs to buy a house but never enough to quit my night job.

After two failed marriages and far too many girlfriends, I fell in love—for what I thought was the last time. We moved in. We planned, loved, fought, and laughed. Then suddenly, after a routine outpatient surgery, she died. Then grief. Grief tortures. It cleaves you tangibly and drops you into an abyss. I plummeted from 205 pounds to 165. I drank. I was at her grave six or seven days a week. When I didn't go I felt guilty. Nothing else mattered. Eventually, with the help of a few great friends and a shrink, I began to climb out of that hole.

I sold my home and took a one-year contract job in Las Vegas; a place I abhorred. But I had a plan: One year in Vegas. One year in Mexico to write and fish.

So I sat on the blanket that used to cover us. A large nylon bag full of mementos from our brief life next to me: Cards. Pictures. Her flight attendant uniform. I talked to her. I used to babble for hours, but I found the more I healed the less I had to say. It was noon on a Monday and the cemetery was empty. The sun shone, the planes descended through it, and I sat.

After some time I called my brother; the person who knew all my secrets and kept them to himself. He'd received hundreds of my calls over the past year and never failed to answer. I told him about the drive and where I was sitting. He took a long beat and gave it to me straight.

"Everybody still dead?" A bit taken aback, I actually looked around. "Yeah."

"Good, if not you should call the *National Enquirer*. Go be with the living, some of them are more interesting." He hung up. I grunted through a tight grin. I was getting better.

I struggled mightily with the decision to move and leave her. And now how to say a goodbye she would never hear.

During that year I had seen an elderly black woman sitting in a low folding chair at the far end of the same row. She came almost as often as I did. She always brought a thermos and a pack of wet wipes. When she had finished her visit, she would take out a wipe, slide off the chair to her knees, clean off a section of the stone. Then kiss it.

Once, after she had left, I walked by. He was a nineteen-year-old male who had been dead five years; the faint outlines of past kisses baked on, surrounding the fresh one like halos.

Back at my vigil, my fiancée beneath me, I faced her inscription. I did the best I could to clean it with my hand. My palms on the short-cropped grass, I bent and kissed her marker; I smelled the sandy earth and felt the warming metal. I pushed up, and at arm's length stared down.

"Goodbye, honey. I won't be back for a while." The "I love you" caught in my throat, but I got it out. I walked to my car with the grit from her stone on my lips.

A SMALL HARVEST OF KISSES

The kiss itself is immortal. It travels from lip to lip, century to century, from age to age. Men and women garner these kisses, offer them to others and then die in turn.

—GUY DE MAUPASSANT, "A Tress of Hair"

The kiss is also a perfect monitor of love. Either we are "into" it, or it sends out a signal of aloofness and lack of feeling. There is no way to camouflage the message present in a kiss. When we give a halfhearted kiss, we will often get the response "Kiss me as if you mean it," from a disgruntled partner. An unshared kiss is worse than no kiss at all. Many times it signals the end of a relationship. As Betty Everett so aptly phrased it in her classic pop song, "It's in his kiss." It is easier to fake sexual pleasure than it is to fake the kiss. Unlike sex, there is nothing to prove in kissing.

—MARCEL DANESI, *The History of the Kiss!:*
The Birth of Popular Culture

When I was in high school in the early Sixties, nice girls didn't go all the way, and most of us wouldn't have known how to anyway. But man, could we kiss! We kissed for hours in the busted-up front seat of a borrowed Chevy which, in motion, sounded like a broken dinette-set; we kissed inventively, clutching our boy-friends from behind as we straddled motorcycles, whose vibra-tions turned our hips to jelly; we kissed extravagantly beside a turtlearium in the park, or at the local rose garden or zoo; we kissed delicately, in waves of sipping and puckering; we kissed torridly, with tongues like hot pokers; we kissed time-lessly, because lovers throughout the ages knew our longing; we kissed wildly, almost painfully, with tough, soul-stealing rigor; we kissed elaborately, as if we were inventing kisses for the first time; we kissed furtively when we met in the hallways between classes; we kissed soulfully in the shadows at concerts, the way we thought musical knights of passion like The Righteous Broth-ers and their ladies did; we kissed articles of clothing or objects belonging to our boyfriends; we kissed our hands when we blew our boyfriends kisses across the street; we kissed our pillows at night pretending they were mates; we kissed shamelessly with the robust sappiness of youth; we kissed as if kissing could save us from ourselves.

At fourteen, just before I went off to summer camp, which is what girls in suburban Pennsylvania did to mark time, my boyfriend, whom my parents did not approve of (wrong reli-gion) and had forbidden me to see, used to walk five miles across town each evening, and climb in through my bedroom window just to kiss me. These were not open-mouthed "French" kisses, which we didn't know about, and they weren't accompanied by groping. They were just earth-stopping, soulful, on-the-ledge-of-adolescence kissing, when you press your lips together and yearn so hard you feel faint. We wrote letters while I was away, and when school started again in the Fall the affair seemed to fade of its accord. But I remember those summer nights, how he would hide in my closet if my parents or brother chanced in, and then kiss me for an hour or so and head back home before it became dark, and I marvel at his determination and the power of a kiss.

—DIANE ACKERMAN, *A Natural History of the Senses*

I did not realize that kissing was a first date taboo. I'm such a sinner.

—ROXANE GAY

ALARACT 350/2011

Sept. 15, 2011

Subject: Clarification Of
Army Standards Of Conduct Policies

1. Reference. Army Regulation 600-20, Army Command Policy, 30 Nov 09.
2. The purpose of this message is to clarify Army policies on Standards of Conduct.

A. Long-standing customs of the service prohibit public displays of affection by Soldiers when in uniform or while in civilian clothes on duty. Soldiers must project an image that leaves no doubt that they live by a common military standard and are responsible to military order and discipline.

B. However, long-standing customs of the service permit modest displays of affection in appropriate circumstances including, but not limited to, weddings, graduations, promotions, retirements or other ceremonies; during the casualty notification/assistance process including funerals; during deployment or welcome home ceremonies; for displays of affection or other physical contact between parents or guardians and children in their charge; or in other circumstances where modest displays of affection are commonly accepted.

—THE U.S. ARMY'S *Journal for Homeland Defense,*
Civil Support and Security Cooperation in
North America (p. 25, September 2011)

Steven returned from the war without lips.

This is quite a shock said his wife Mary who had spent the last six months knitting sweaters and avoiding a certain grocery store where a certain young man worked and looked at her in that certain way. I expected lips. Dead or alive, but with lips.

Steven went into the living room where his old favorite chair stood, neatly dusted and unused. I-can-eat-like-normal, he said in a strange halted clacking tone due to the plastic disc that covered and protected what was left of his mouth like the end of a pacifier. The-doctors-are-going-to-put-new-skin-on-in-a-few-weeks-anyway. Skin-from-my-palm. He lifted up his hand and looked at it. That-will-work, I-guess, he said. It-just-won't-be-quite-the-same.

No, said Mary, it won't. That bomb, she said, standing on the other side of the chair, you know it took the last real kiss from you forever, and as far as I can remember, that kiss was supposed to be mine.

—AIMEE BENDER, "What You Left in the Ditch"
from *The Girl in the Flammable Skirt: Stories*

I want, she said, moving into position, un beso.

And before he could say anything she was on him.

The first feel of woman's body pressing against yours—who among us can ever forget that? And that first real kiss—well, to be honest, I've forgotten both of these firsts, but Oscar never would.

For a second he was in disbelief. This is it, this is really it! Her lips plush and pliant, and her tongue pushing into his mouth. And then there were lights all around them and he thought I'm going to transcend! Transcendence is miiine! But then he realized that the two plainclothes who had pulled them over—who both looked like they'd been raised on high-G planets, and whom we'll call Solomon Grundy and Gorilla Grod for simplicity's sake—were beaming their flashlights into the car. And who was standing behind them, looking in on the scene inside the car with an expression of sheer murder? Why, the capitán of course. Ybón's boyfriend!

—JUNOT DÍAZ, *The Brief Wondrous Life of Oscar Wao*

His heart beat faster and faster as Daisy's white face came up to his own. He knew that when he kissed this girl, and forever wed his unutterable visions to her perishable breath, his mind would never romp again like the mind of God. So he waited, listening for a moment longer to the tuning fork that had been struck upon a star. Then he kissed her. At his lips' touch she blossomed like a flower and the incarnation was complete.

—F. SCOTT FITZGERALD, *The Great Gatsby*

"I think it's perfectly sweet of you," she declared, "and I'll get up again," and she sat with him on the side of the bed. She also said she would give him a kiss if he liked, but Peter did not know what she meant, and he held out his hand expectantly.

"Surely you know what a kiss is?" she asked, aghast.

"I shall know when you give it to me," he replied stiffly, and not to hurt his feelings she gave him a thimble.

"Now," said he, "shall I give you a kiss?" and she replied with a slight primness, "If you please." She made herself rather cheap by inclining her face toward him, but he merely dropped an acorn button into her hand, so she slowly returned her face to where it had been before, and said nicely that she would wear his kiss on the chain around her neck. It was lucky that she did put it on that chain, for it was afterwards to save her life.

—J. M. BARRIE, *Peter Pan*

NO KISS FORGOTTEN; it resides in the memory as in the flesh, and so Katya many times felt the press of Marcus Kidder's warm mouth on hers in the days and especially in the nights following. And her heartbeat quickened in protest: How could you! Kiss him! That old man! Kiss him! Let him put his arms around you and kiss you and kiss him back! The old man's mouth and Katya Spivak's mouth! How could you.

—JOYCE CAROL OATES, *A Fair Maiden*

The kiss of shame was more than just a parody of the kiss of peace and a symbol of the heretics' solidarity. The physical act of putting one's lips to the anus, buttocks or genitalia revealed other attributes of the witch sect and the character of the witch. It is interesting that descriptions of the *osculum infame* give an alternative site of kissing: the feet. This detail has its origins in the Gospel episode in which a sinner, usually identified as Mary Magdalene, washed Christ's feet with her tears. After she had dried them with her hair and anointed them with perfume, she kissed them. The whole ritual was one of adoration and reverence, and the kiss element of it became incorporated into the rituals of greeting the Pope. The kiss offered by Mary Magdalene to Jesus, king of the Jews, also reflected the kiss given by Samuel to Saul after he had anointed him king of Israel, a kiss which found its way into European coronation ceremonies. In this sense the kiss could be interpreted as an act of fealty and honour. Alternatively, the kissing of feet could be used as a sign of humility not to sovereigns, but to God.

—JONATHAN DURRANT, "The Osculum Infame:
Heresy, Secular Culture and the Image of the Witches' Sabbath"
from *The Kiss in History* (Karen Harvey, ed., p. 43)

They lay listening. Can you do it? When the time comes? When the time comes there will be no time. Now is the time. Curse God and die. What if it doesnt fire? It has to fire. What if it doesn't fire? Could you crush that beloved skull with a rock? Is there such a being within you of which you know nothing? Can there be? Hold him in your arms. Just so. The soul is quick. Pull him toward you. Kiss him. Quickly.

—CORMAC McCARTHY, *The Road*

He back in my mouth before I can say bad man don't kiss. Sucking my tongue, moving his lips over my lips, tongue on tongue, dancing it and making me do it back. He is making me think like a faggot.

—Aw, look at you. You just giggled like a school girl. There may be hope for you yet.

Lip on top of lip, lip turned on the side licking me in the mouth, tongue on top of tongue, underneath tongue, lips sucking my tongue, and I open my eye and see him two eye close tight. That moan come from him not me. I reach up and squeeze him nipples but not hard, I still don't know hot from hurt. But he moan and now he taking him tongue down my chest to my nipples and my navel leaving a wet trail that feel cold even though him tongue warm. New York spying me do this? I spy what do you spy? B A T T Y with a tight needle-eye. Outside the window is five floor up but I don't know. Too high for the window washer or pigeon or whoever climbing the wall although nobody would be climbing no wall. Nobody can see but the sky. But Air Jamaica going fly right by and Josey going see me. The man tickle my navel with him tongue and I grab him head. He look up for second and smile and the hair pass through my fingers so thin, so soft, so brown. Hair that make you sound white when you describe it.

—Come back, fucker.

—MARLON JAMES, *A Brief History of Seven Killings*

"Let's not go on with the medical lesson," she said.

"No," he said. "This is going to be a lesson in love."

Then he pulled down the sheet and she not only did not object but kicked it away from the bunk with a rapid movement of her feet because she could no longer bear the heat. Her body was undulant and elastic, much more serious than it appeared when dressed, with its own scent of a forest animal, which distinguished her from all the other women in the world. Defenseless in the light, she felt a rush of blood surge up to her face, and the only way she could think of to hide it was to throw her arms around her husband's neck and give him a hard, thorough kiss that lasted until they were both gasping for breath.

He was aware that he did not love her. He had married her because he liked her haughtiness, her seriousness, her strength, and also because of some vanity on his part, but as she kissed him for the first time he was sure there would be no obstacle to their inventing true love. They did not speak of it that first night, when they spoke of everything until dawn, nor would they ever speak of it. But in the long run, neither of them had made a mistake.

—GABRIEL GARCÍA MÁRQUEZ,
Love in the Time of Cholera

"You, Al," said Phil. "I really value your input."

"Well, sir," said Al, the mirror-faced Advisor, flattered to have been asked. "In my view? Love is one of the most outstanding experiences a human being can undergo. When we love someone, wow, we just feel so super about being with them and sharing such experiences as our feelings and emotions, not to mention hopes and dreams we might possess. The feeling we get from that interaction is for the most part the most pleasant one we can ever do. And commitment, that commitment we feel, is the strongest bond we can subject ourselves to."

"I so much agree!" said Phil. "I love love. All Outer Hornerites love love, but the sort of love we love to love is of the gentle connubial sort between man and wife, not this sleazy proposed love between unwed sweaty lusters! But clearly, there can be no marriage between Inner and Outer Hornerite! That would be like a swan marrying a worm! And why would a swan do that? They could not even kiss, what with a worm having no lips and a swan merely a beak! Therefore this propositioning letter does not reek of love, but of lust, not of marriage, but of unseemly sweaty trysts between disparate types. Trysts of sly barter! Like a transaction! She gives me what I want and I give her what she wants, and it is all grunts grunts grunts and no gentle smiles between grunts at all! It is all business! She is willing to sell herself, this harlot. Willing to sell herself to the leader of the enemy of her people! Please step forward! Step forward whichever harlot wrote this!"

—GEORGE SAUNDERS,
The Brief and Frightening Reign of Phil

"Here," she said, "in this here place, we flesh; flesh that weeps, laughs; flesh that dances on bare feet in grass. Love it. Love it hard. Yonder they do not love your flesh. They despise it. They don't love your eyes; they'd just as soon pick em out. No more do they love the skin on your back. Yonder they flay it. And O my people they do not love your hands. Those they only use, tie, bind, chop off and leave empty. Love your hands! Love them. Raise them up and kiss them. Touch others with them, pat them together, stroke them on your face 'cause they don't love that either. You got to love it, you! And no, they ain't in love with your mouth. Yonder, out there, they will see it broken and break it again. What you say out of it they will not heed. What you scream from it they do not hear. What you put into it to nourish your body they will snatch away and give you leavins instead. No, they don't love your mouth. You got to love it. This is flesh I'm talking about here. Flesh that needs to be loved. Feet that need to rest and to dance; backs that need support; shoulders that need arms, strong arms I'm telling you. And O my people, out yonder, hear me, they do not love your neck unnoosed and straight. So love your neck; put a hand on it, grace it, stroke it and hold it up. And all your inside parts that they'd just as soon slop for hogs, you got to love them. The dark, dark liver—love it, love it and the beat and beating heart, love that too. More than eyes or feet. More than lungs that have yet to draw free air. More than your life-holding womb and your life-giving private parts, hear me now, love your heart. For this is the prize."

—TONI MORRISON, *Beloved*

She leaned down and looked at his lifeless face and Leisel kissed her best friend, Rudy Steiner, soft and true on his lips. He tasted dusty and sweet. He tasted like regret in the shadows of trees and in the glow of the anarchist's suit collection. She kissed him long and soft, and when she pulled herself away, she touched his mouth with her fingers . . . She did not say goodbye.

—MARKUS ZUSAK, *The Book Thief*

. . . She was a little dark, and her dark eyebrows were narrow but thick and defined, with a little arch like a V pointing upward in the middle of each one. And her eyes, closed, were wide-set. But it was her mouth that transfixed Parnell. It was broad and full, her lips a little dry and cracked, and now parted in death he could only imagine how expressive it must have been when she was at home, with family, and uninhibited by her shyness, how much joy she must have given to her mother and father, how much they must have hoped for her.

It was the hint of exotic in her features that began to sink into him now. What exotic locale they suggested he could not imagine, but someplace different. It was not the look of a gypsy. Until the woman with parrot fever, which ended it all, his father had often embalmed and buried gypsies; he had a friendship with the old gypsy queen's son. He'd buried the queen, in that grand ceremony they'd conducted down 8th Street to the old cemetery west of town, Rose Hill. But she was not a tipsy. Her name, now he remembered, was Littleton, that was fitting. Constance Littleton, they called her Connie. Little Connie Littleton, here alone with Parnell. He leaned down and kissed her lips. Dry as desiccated clay. No give there. No, there was the faintest. She was not entirely cold. Still fresh in death, still sweet in passing. Still between the living and the dead, her spirit not entirely removed.

—BRAD WATSON, *The Heaven of Mercury*

"It is through closure that openness is divided into things. Without closure we would be lost in a sea of openness: a sea without character and without form." Closure is about defining limits, and while some of those limits are negative and constricting, they are also the basis for our reality: "Closure is responsible . . . for our being able to experience a sunrise over a field of corn; or hear the sound of a log fire and the warmth that it brings; it is closure that makes possible the kiss of a lover or the pain of injury."

—HILARY LAWSON, *Closure: A Story of Everything*

"A kiss may not be the truth but it is what we wish were true."

—STEVE MARTIN

(as Harris Telemacher in *L.A. Story*)

KISS KISS BANG BANG

Téa Obreht and Dan Sheehan

Returning from a recent trip, Dan Sheehan and I got wrapped up in talking about the most iconic kisses of the silver screen. We had just surrendered all attempts to celebrate our fourth anniversary to help my family host a massive dinner party. Frenzied preparations had left us exhausted, more than a little hung over, and battling the onslaught of spring colds while we meandered through the bowels of Washington's teeming Union Station. We were separated on a packed train bound for New York's Penn Station, and were forced to continue our debate by iMessage from several rows away.

TO: All right, so what are your criteria?
DS: Well, deciding on the single best anything is a fool's errand, damn near impossible, so instead I propose three categories: Sexiest Kiss; Most Romantic Kiss; and Strangest/Most Sinister Kiss.

TO: For a moment there I misread that as "Sexist Kiss" and thought: that's going to be a damn long list. How do you define romantic? And does sexiest mean it must lead to a love scene?

DS: A romantic movie kiss is one where the other background aspects of the situation don't overwhelm the romance. So if the ratio of grief/lust/hypnosis to good old-fashioned love is greater than 50:50, then the kiss in question has been compromised and will have to be categorized elsewhere. Sexy kisses can lead to sex, but don't necessarily have to. These are my arbitrary rules.

TO: Sounds fair. Strangest/Most Sinister seems a broad category. It's obviously one that only comes into its own upon second viewing.

DS: Fun fact about that category: it was created so I could shoehorn in Michael Corleone's "I know it was you, Fredo" kiss of death, administered to his traitorous brother as confetti rains down on them at a wedding reception in *The Godfather: Part II*. However, I'm sure there are other worthy examples.

TO: Mostly between family members—my Strangest/Most Sinister award definitely goes to Leia kissing Luke in *The Empire Strikes Back*. This is one leery red herring. It's meant to be titillating. It's meant to provoke jealousy in Han Solo. Then Luke puts his hands behind his head in peacocking triumph. But she's his sister! The writers already know it, and once we do it makes all subsequent viewings extremely uncomfortable. Sidebar: there's a pretty steamy train kiss happening at my 3 o'clock right now . . . your 5 p.m. . . .

DS: There is some serious steam rising there all right. But yes, incest kisses in family movies definitely belong in that category. I'm thinking of Marty McFly and his mother in *Back to the Future*.

TO: Another skincrawling one. As is the kiss from *Big*. The early 80s really were a bizarre free-for-all in this regard.

DS: God yeah, you'd never get away with *Big* nowadays. Going deeper down the unpleasant kisses rabbit hole, how about Jack Nicholson embracing a corpse-ghost in *The Shining*?

TO: That almost made my list. Oh! You know what? I stand by my Luke & Leia pick, but now feel obliged to give a shout-out to Joaquin Phoenix's repressed priest throwing the lips on a recently dead Kate Winslet in *Quills*. This is one of my favorite films, not least of all because of their chemistry throughout. But then she's killed in what can only be termed a literary sexcapade gone horribly wrong, and he's so guilt-stricken he ends up hallucinating a sexual encounter with her shrouded corpse on a church altar.

DS: Christ almighty—that might warrant its own special category. We'd have to use the Internet café computers for that research, though.

TO: Moving on, then. Where do you stand on Most Romantic Kiss?

DS: I'll entertain arguments for *Casablanca* or *Lost in Translation* or *Brokeback Mountain*, but for me, it's gotta be the climactic kiss between a plucky, trash-compacting, earthbound robot and hopeless romantic, and his sleek, technologically advanced, no-nonsense girlfriend at the end of *WALL-E* . . .

TO: Eve!

DS: Gets me every time.

TO: That song, though.

DS: And the song is the clincher. Till then WALL-E's amnesia threatens to tip the grief-romance balance. But just when you think that all is lost, that the memory of their magical robo-courtship has been permanently deleted, those magnificent heartstring-tuggers at Pixar pull it out of the fire.

TO: Pulling it out of the fire is crucial for romantic category kisses, I think. Nothing worse than waiting all movie long for something that suddenly seems unlikely to catch fire. Mine: ex-con Al Pacino has spent the better part of *Frankie and Johnny* trying to convince diner waitress Michelle Pfeiffer that they're meant for each other—she's reluctant for a whole host of very good reasons we don't yet know, but the end of a hard-won first date finds them roaming the Flower District, where Al makes his overture in a series of ever-simplifying gestures while the rising musical score drowns out his voice. Their first real kiss happens at the crescendo, just as a delivery guy throws open the cargo bay behind them, suddenly revealing a brilliant Eden of violet flowers. It's one for the books.

DS: I'm ashamed to say I've never even heard of *Frankie and Johnny*, but I've just watched the scene in question and it's a hell of a kiss. Pacino as offbeat romantic lead is a very underrated Pacino.

TO: Pacino is the only one making a repeat appearance on this list so far—so I think it's safe to say he's an underrated kisser overall. Of course, one would rather have my kind of Pacino kiss than yours, I think. Because of death.

DS: Sure. That's the strange beauty of the Pacino kiss though: you never know what you're gonna get.

TO: 50% chance it's death. 50% chance it's some other thing. 100% chance that it will involve shouting, either way.

DS: If you can't handle the shouting, you don't deserve Al's kisses.

TO: Al was very close to featuring on my Sexiest Kiss list, actually, in *Sea of Love*. But he was defeated.

DS: *Sea of Love*, now there's a dangerously sexy film. I'll never understand why they stopped making erotic thrillers. Hands down the best cinematic genre.

TO: Sometimes extinction is senseless, Dan. And unjust.

DS: They truly are the dinosaurs of contemporary Hollywood.

TO: The best we can hope for is that Steven Spielberg will resurrect them as he did the dinosaurs.

DS: Now that you mention Spielberg, the lack of sex in his films is pretty remarkable. He should have spent more time with Michael Douglas.

TO: Maybe he's saving it all up for one sweet, ultimate erotic thriller to rule them all.

DS: We can only hope. Michael's not getting any younger. So if not *Sea of Love*, what then?

TO: So Sexiest Kiss, for me, has always been a steady favorite. Sure, a few contenders have threatened to unseat it over the years—*Brokeback Mountain* ranks in this category for me; *The Piano* is pretty high up, too. But for all it's an otherwise problematic film, there's just no beating Daniel Day-Lewis and Madeline Stowe's romantic interlude in *The Last of the Mohicans*. That whole film is basically foreplay for their epic make-out on the eve of the big battle—to the extent that, when they find each other at the fire while those amazing violins play, they don't even have to be coy about what it is they're heading up to the guard tower to do.

DS: Nice. The sexiness really does ratchet up when a couple are trying to evade death together. In that spirit, I'm gonna have to go with the Sarah Connor/Kyle Reese motel room kiss toward the end of *The Terminator*. By this point, the relentless T-800 cyborg has been stalking future mother of the resistance Sarah and time-traveling soldier Reese through the streets of Los Angeles for a good half hour and they're at their wits' end. In a moment of vulnerability, Reese confesses that back in the future year of 2029, he fell madly in love with a picture of Sarah. As you do. Then, as he angrily shoves homemade pipe bombs into a duffel bag, mad at himself for revealing too much, Sarah moves in for the kiss. If what transpires doesn't get your motor running, you're as asexual as the Terminator. Or one of Spielberg's films.

TO: I have to tell you something. I have never seen *The Terminator*. I know you love it. I know you paid $3 to rescue a VHS tape of it from our bodega, where it was serving as a display rung for boxes of Ritter Sport, and that you've since hidden it among our books. Sometimes, when you say something that sounds like a film-line and look at me knowingly, I suspect you must be quoting *The Terminator*, but I can never know for sure.

DS: Everything I know about love, sex, relationships, time travel, cyborgs, and pipe bombs, I learned from *The Terminator*.

TO: Then never mind. I've seen *The Terminator*.

CONTAGION

Roxana Robinson

n a foreign country, everything is strange. You walk the streets like a child, trying to understand the stream of newness pouring over you.

I was in Kyoto to see the gardens, which are marvelously strange, and unlike anything in Europe. We went one day to a fancy hotel to see a vertical garden: an interior wall, planted in mosses and orchids and vines. We couldn't get close, because it was in a reception room where a private event was being held. We stood in the doorway, in the back.

The room was full of seated well-dressed people. They were all watching the stage, which held a young couple and a middle-aged woman. The older woman stood at a podium, with a book and a microphone. The young man wore a dark suit and the young woman wore a long white dress. Clearly they were getting married. The officiant spoke and they answered, in a formal ritual exchange. I couldn't understand the words, but I understood the import, the grave message of commitment and responsibility.

When it was over the groom turned to the bride. He was much taller than she, and he leaned down toward her. He put his hands on her shoulders, moving his face close to hers. But the bride shrank away, her body dropping, her head turning to one side, refusing him.

It was a mystery. What was this strange ritual, the approach, withdrawal, public rejection? For a moment they were motionless on the stage, his hands poised over her shoulders, her hands behind her back, face turned utterly away.

Then I became aware of something—movement and sound—that was rippling through the audience. It started in the front and ran softly through the guests in their elegant clothes. It reached all the way to the back to the foreigners in the doorway. It was a ripple of laughter.

The bride had got the giggles. Her body shrank because she couldn't hold herself sober. Her body had given way to that joyful explosion that laughter makes inside us. As her groom approached, something had taken her over. And that something had taken over the audience. Everyone felt the visceral recognition of this private, intimate eruption. Everyone was giggling quietly, remembering how delight takes over your body. We all gave way, remembering how gravity is only one side of something else, something that can't be controlled, something that makes us helpless and unrestrained and joyful.

The giggle spread quietly through us, quick and subversive. We were invaded by laughter. Then, like a wave, it smoothed itself out and vanished into the sand. The bride straightened, her face turned serious. The giggle had moved through her. She straightened and looked up at the groom. Her face was now calm and radiant.

Again he leaned toward her, now hesitant, aware that anything could happen, any kind of explosion might pull them apart.

But it did not. He brought his mouth to hers, she lifted her lips, and they kissed. We watched, remembering that, too.

KISS

Honor Moore

A laugh on the landline. I went outside so I could think. I couldn't think. What do you want to do with me? I want to take you out to dinner. A week before, a party flirt across a room. Stranger, though I knew his name. The April evening goes dark as we don't eat, but when I spear pale green melon, he puts it in his mouth. We walk, dark, then arms and shock, tongue the ocean and suddenly my mouth was small. A wave that takes you so fast under, it could kill you. We had crossed a street. Gone inside. Not home, not anyone's home. The whole time standing, as if I were pliable. Your tongue, he said, put it in my mouth. I had forgotten to move and I did what he asked, as if there were a way to eternity or it was important to tell very hot from very cold. That summer, in a sleeper alone on a night train through the Alps, vibration of wheel on rail, all-night shudder as if it were him beneath me, as if we had continued. April. Seventeen years ago, almost to the day.

GENESIS

Christopher Merrill

D*on't stop*, she said as he poured from the watering can the keys to houses she had never visited, drawers she could not unlock, cars reserved for others. Then coins from countries that appeared on none of her itineraries—Ukraine and Indonesia and Iran, not to mention Argentina and Brazil. And hoop earrings she would not be caught dead in, glass beads from a necklace worn by someone else, a silver brooch that made her heart ache. *Don't stop*, she said when there was nothing left—and so he filled the can with water to sprinkle over the objects spread like seeds on the dining room table. One by one they sprouted into new lines of argument, and as they grew she raised her hands above her head, crying, *Don't stop.*

What did they seek in the storeroom, garden, and bedroom? What drew them night after night to a shuttered house on the bluff above the

sea, vowing to repair the damage caused by the shifting earth—cracks in the adobe, loosened tiles in the kitchen? Kiss the feet, the hand, the mouth: this was their credo, adapted from a text translated by an adjunct from the valley. *Marry word and deed*, he told them at the final exam. Weeks passed before they got his little joke, by which time he had taken another job out of state. They didn't try to find him: there was too much to do. The rains were heavier than usual, uprooted trees slid down the bluff, and while they debated whether to reinforce the foundation the earth gave way in a wall of mud that covered the road, burying an empty tractor trailer and an armored car returning from the casino. They had no title to the house riding out to sea. The one song they knew had something to do with desire.

Oscula—this was the word on the tip of the tongue of the woman who refused to travel farther down the coast without assurances that she could film whatever she liked. The soldiers patrolling the beach were negotiating the terms of their surrender to the insurgents, who had invited her to join them for the march to the capital, and she was surprised by her mixture of emotions at the prospect of peace. The enticements of the sun and sea were parceled out among the families gathered on the shore, the fishermen lining the jetty, and the feverish man pulling a barrel full of monkeys down the boardwalk. He stopped to wipe his brow and saw, riding at anchor in the harbor, a ghost ship laden with medicine and provisions. There was an old man collecting coils of rope in the wrack and rocks below the hotel, which had been attacked on the first day of the war. How it remained open throughout the siege was a mystery to everyone but the manager, who cautioned guests not to leave their satchels under the table, or else they would lose their money. Wiggle your hips, throw something out—it was all the same to him. Diamonds vanished from the market, and no one seemed to mind. The soldiers laid down their weapons and removed their boots, posing for the camera. *Kiss me,* the woman said, remembering—and they did.

A MOTION OF PLEASURE

J. Mae Barizo

I.

Imagine a small town in Southern Ontario with two rivers running through it. Church spires, cobblestone, Carolinian forest. It is the early eighties and besides the Iroquois children in your school, you are the only girl of color: brown skin, black eyes, bowl cut. The locals think your father is First Nation, they sometimes give him tax-free gas when he fills up the tank of his Soviet-era olive-green Lada, the first car your parents own.

The snow is so bright you have to squint when you walk out into it, a blinding white. Your father gets pneumonia because he grew up on an island in the Pacific; he and your mother emigrated to Canada when you were only a speck on the horizon. You are born in that northern country so your first memories are of snow: your skinny father building an igloo big enough for both of you to sit in. The sky is white, the streets are white, the people are white. The first girl you love, the year you turn four, has white breasts you reach toward, laughing. Only later do you realize it was your mother's breasts you were thinking of, the mother who worked so hard in your first year of life that you barely saw her; you were relegated to a Filipino granny who fed you from a bottle, your baby lips pursed.

II.

Your first kiss is with a Haitian-Canadian boy from Montreal who has a French name that sounds aristocratic; he is not. He kisses you in a stark white racquetball court in the middle of a game and you drop your racket; the sound of it reverberating through the soundproof room.

III.

The man leaning over you is concentrating on your left breast, the sound of Mozart ribbons through the air. His tongue flutters over your nipple as the rest of your body rises. You clutch his shoulder then slap his face, your teeth on his white skin. Months later you still remember his mouth, approaching and retreating.

IV.

The midwife tells you to think about the sea. A white beach with palm trees; docile, white-tipped waves. "I don't fucking like the beach!" you tell her through clenched teeth. "Breathe," she croons. "Where do you want to go, then, let's go to that place," she says with her gentle West Indian accent, taking your hand in hers. "A field of snow," you say as another torrent of pain rips through. Everything goes white.

V.

A wail slices through the air and you come to. "She's losing blood," you hear a nurse say, and at once there is a trio of people congregating in front of you, looking between your legs. You are suddenly conscious of tears running down the side of your face, you are inhaling tears as you breathe, your tears are falling into the sides of your mouth, you taste the salt of your own tears. You see a pair of metal shears, severing the cord that has attached her to you. The tiny mouth won't stop wailing, the tiny fists beat the air—first contact with the outside world. Her body is covered with your blood and then her body is pressed against your body, her mouth clamping onto your breast, a wet animal warmth.

VI.

A mother's milk, the first inherent ardor.

"Imagine a small town with two rivers running through it," you tell the child, the whites of her eyes shifting back and forth as her mind moves.

"Her voice was like a line from an old black and white Jean-Luc Godard movie, filtering in just beyond the frame of my consciousness," writes Haruki Murakami.

"I can't remember kissing someone for such a long time," you say to him, your mouth on his eyelid.

"A field of snow," you shout before the pain rips through.

The child's melon-pink mouth, rooting.

"Everything," Kant says, "exists only in our mind attended by a motion of pleasure."

KISS, BOUNCE, GRACE

Steven Church

There is this different kind of kiss I know, one layered with memory and associations, one containing the promise of forgiveness. Like a key to a lock I cannot see. Unique from the others, this kiss lands loud and hard at first and leaves a blue mark. But it always bounces elsewhere. My father used to bring the stains home on the back of his thighs or his lower back, near the kidneys.

He taught me that this kiss is sometimes not planted with lips but by a brief meeting of racquetball and back, sometimes ball and thigh, or ball and eye, gifting you a bluish purple bruise the same size and shape as the ball itself—as if it has left its shadow on your skin, a shadow of a memory.

This is not the part I crave. Not the pain. But maybe the paint, the mark.

———

It is the kiss of ball to wall that I'm after. It's the bounce off the concrete to the blur, the breath and noise. You know the kiss is good because of the sound. And here, in the moment, it's all about the sound and the sensory rush. When you hit the blue ball good with the sweet spot of the racket, there's a special noise it makes, a kind of hollow *pong-whoop*, and you know the shot will be hard and fast, and you can almost feel it reverberate in your chest like a bass drum; when you cock the hammer, racket raised over your head, and bring it down hard and fast, transferring all the momentum to your wrist and the racket head, you feel like motherfuckin' Zeus unleashing lightning bolts from your fist. When you hit it good, the racket transfers all your angst, all those spinning thoughts and self-doubt into the blue ball and sends it slamming into the wall. But when you miss the moves and catch the kiss wrong, the shot falls flat and sends a shock-shiver up your arm like a tuning fork smacked on concrete. It rings your bell a bit and humbles you, confronts you with your failures to follow the bounce.

This kiss still reminds me. This bounce. This is what I try to track.

Imagine, if you will, entering a bright white windowless room, the only entrance a white door, smaller than a normal door, with a tiny fogged-up plastic window. The side walls are rimmed around the bottom with the black scuff marks of sneakers, a cloud of impact that rises up and fades into shadows of blue ball scuff. Black to blue. And back again. It looks like someone has tried desperately to climb the walls. The occasional constellation of cracks in the front wall, combined with decades of chipped paint, create subtle valleys, dips deep enough that they can ricochet the ball off at odd angles and keep you guessing about your worthiness. And this game is all about understanding the angles of bounce. It's about patience. And forgiveness of your sins of the eye and hand.

In this game, this play, this dance, the ultimate kiss is the kill shot. Rackets are rated according to their kill shot potential. And each shot has its own sound, as significant as its force and speed and location. A kill shot sounds sharp, quick, like gunfire, and then it dies, usually as the ball dribbles out across the floor, impossible to return; and sometimes, if you hit the ball directly into the spot where the wall meets the floor, it makes a kind of hollow pop like a balloon and sputters to stop against a side wall. If you put all your pain into it, a kill shot can save you. And sometimes after a long rally, a rollicking volley of shots, the ball will feel warm to the touch, as if its chemistry is beginning to break down and you think it might melt in your hand. You've seen a ball split like a melon rind, too tired of the pounding.

Thus I arrive in my half-awake state, seven a.m. on a Sunday at my local gym. There in that temple of noise, I turn my arm into a whipping noodle with a racket attached, and the blue orb, unleashed, seems to hover and glow, lit from within, as it zips and bounces beneath the early morning light-emitting diode of the racquetball court—the hardwood and concrete church of chipped paint and cracked walls, the holey ceiling and half-ass patch job, piles of paint chips in the corner, shed like scales before your eyes. Sometimes the ball comes back to you dusted with white as it takes part of the wall with each kiss.

I play alone these days. Fifteen minutes to pray before my cardio time. Fifteen minutes of lightning and thunder. And it *is* an odd kind of meditation for me. A rhythmic trance where my body moves and my mind follows the bounce, leaping from one thought to another, all of them contained within the court, each one coming fast like a blue ball, and all I have to do is send it back hard or let it pass. It's hard to explain the synesthetic rush of such worship.

The blue ball flies fast, daring you to keep up.

On Sunday mornings when I was a kid, my father used to take us for donuts and drop us off at the church where my mother worked running youth programs. Then he'd drive to his own places of worship, the racquetball courts or a bar called the Sanctuary where he sometimes took us for the all-you-can-eat taco bar after we got home from church. When we asked him why he didn't come with us to church, he'd say, "I did my time."

Dad's religion was a different sort, the kind practiced regularly on racquetball courts, the kind that sent him home some Sundays with those round purple bruises. After the divorce, my brother and I would often go with him after school and lift weights or kill time in the hot tub and sauna while he played a few games with his friends; and I can still recall the loud ruckus of those days as their noisy kisses echoed off the walls and filled the small gym lobby.

When the games were finished we'd all head across the street to the Mexican restaurant where my brother and I would order a Roy Rogers and a Shirley Temple and my dad and his friends would drink beer and eat chips and salsa and queso dip and they would talk the language of men, a tongue we had yet to master but wanted desperately to learn. I think of my father every time I step onto a racquetball court and can still hear his voice booming off the walls. It's a kind of reconnection, an intimacy through noise and sense memory—each visit like a trip back home. The ball. The court. The noise. And my father.

Still we bounce, each thought leaving a mark.

This gym is also the poet's gym, the place near the railroad tracks where you might find the local Fresno poets Chuck Hanzlicek or, before they died, John Vineburg and the Pulitzer Prize winner and former poet laureate Philip Levine. This valley is Levine's valley in many ways, forever elevated by his love for a misunderstood place, his poetry, and his personality. This gym is his gym, the place I used to jokingly call "Senior Center Point," this gym with the leaking ceiling that can't handle the infrequent rains. This gym with its dead-spot wood floors that slope off to the side. This place is now my temple of visceral and sensual escape. This palace of kisses. Racket to ball. Ball to wall. Ball to floor. Bounce. Bounce. This gym and its rhythmic flow of noisy prayer. Everything echoes and reverberates until you are awash in the sound, the slap, the pong; and physics even bends to the glory, and you can watch sound try to catch up with the speed of light as the ball, hit well, leaps off the wall and the noise of its impact chases a split second behind. Part of you watches this happen and understands this is the way that a metaphor works—the vehicle leaping off the white page, the meaning trailing behind and echoing off the walls.

As far as I know Phil Levine didn't play racquetball, but he was known as an excellent tennis player, someone who understood the angles and appreciated the bounce, someone who played to win and didn't take it easy on lesser opponents. His modest house sits surrounded by large eucalyptus and redwood trees, just a mile or so from the gym where I now play and run on the elliptical machine; and he claimed to have written almost all of his books there in that house. His widow, Fran, still lives in the house year-round. I've known both of them for years and was once lucky enough to live there while Phil and Franny split time in their Brooklyn apartment. This was after my marriage had crumbled under pressures both inevitable and unpredictable; my kids spent half the week with me and we were all trying to negotiate a new life. Many days I felt like a terrible father and a failure; but Phil and Franny opened their home and welcomed my children and me without judgment. In the mornings, after I dropped the kids off at school, I'd often retreat to the gym for a few games of racquetball with friends. My therapist had suggested that I get some regular exercise as a way to combat the waves of anxiety and depression that seemed to wash over me at times; and I could not deny that I found deep solace in the simple bounce of a blue ball. I found some peace through the noise of racquet-ball and release through the thunder and lightning. And I'd come home spent, emptied, and sit at Philip Levine's desk—an old door propped up on a couple of filing cabinets—and I'd write in Phil's office, surrounded by his books, experiencing a kind of intimacy with genius that comes along rarely in life. Later, for dinner, I'd cook from Fran's recipe books for my children and imagine that everything would be okay. It is not an exaggeration to say that the Levine house felt like a spiritual place, inhabited by the benevolent ghosts of art and poetry and jazz. Some days I'd flip through Phil's shelves of classic jazz albums and drop a needle on Bird or Coltrane, Rollins or Blakey, maybe Miles Davis and *Kind of Blue*. I didn't write poems in that hallowed house, but I wrote essays, mostly, things like this that ramble and move by digression and association, essays that bounce with associative fervor, because that's the way my mind moves most naturally—pinging off something small, the idea of a kiss, to something larger like racquetball and religion, recovery, and back to this simple memory: *When she greets you, Franny Levine, a small woman with an impossibly bright smile and soft eyes magnified by her glasses, will reach up to you and cup your face in her hands; she'll hold you there, look you in the eye, never blinking, and kiss you square on the lips or maybe on the side of your face, keeping you in her embrace for a second or two—and this small gesture, this mark, is filled with more kindness and love than most people get in a day or a week or a month. This is no coldly formal European side-kiss. This is something bigger, deeper, the difference between a fountain and a well. She will reach out, bridging the abyss between any two humans, and offer this kiss, this true gift, this brief meeting of spheres, and you'll feel like a balloon being inflated, and believe quite suddenly in the possibility of grace.*

FRUIT

Cameron Dezen Hammon

Hail Mary, full of grace,

We shouldn't have and we almost didn't. We were one floor below my sleeping lover, and the sleeping classmates we both loved. Graduation day was coming. Who was sleeping? We weren't. And if they were, I suppose I'll never know.

the Lord is with thee;

I like to think they were. I like to think we were alone in that dusty apartment, three a.m. In that sad, crumbling building, like two people on the moon are alone. Blood rushed in our ears. It canceled out all nightsound. No cicadas sang in the wiry trees. No wind swell. No bobcat or coyote. If there was anything outside the tight link of us we didn't care.

blessed art thou amongst women, and blessed is the fruit of thy womb,
   Jesus.

We stood apart first, then closer, then finally nose to nose, so close we could smell the heat of our bodies. We can still smell it. We offered the broken fruit of our mouths and then knelt like penitents. What is it but worship when we yield our mouths like this?

   Holy Mary, Mother of God,

We shouldn't have and we almost didn't. We kept stoking that weak pulse long after our bodies were in different cities, long after any chance to complete the circuit we'd built was lost. Yet we still think about it. We still write about it. We fill blank page after blank page.

   pray for us sinners, now and at the hour of our death.

We saw ourselves from the distance of the old people we will someday be. We were young and beautiful then. We were an unexpected, brief passion. We loved the sadness because it made us work. We marveled at the sight—the dropped crutches, the leprosy, cured. We reached for the hem of the garment—a frayed concert T-shirt, a pair of dirty cutoffs. Our mouths hung open at the miracle—the power of one illicit kiss in the middle of the night.

   Amen.

FIRE THE ANGEL

Martín Espada

My brother called on a Friday night: *If you want to see him, come now.* I bought a plane ticket from Boston to San Francisco. On Saturday, there was a blizzard. The flight was canceled. Frank Espada died on Sunday, February 16, 2014.

I arrived the next day, drove my mother to the mortuary, and wrote a check for my father's cremation. The white box of ashes sits on a chair in my study. Atop the box there is a snapshot of my father at age seventeen, in his baseball uniform, kicking high in the air and reaching back with his right hand, almost to the ground, in the action of whipping a baseball home.

I would talk to the box of ashes. I missed the hour of his death, my last chance to say something meaningful in his ear, to lean over and kiss his forehead.

There were no more kisses once I reached junior high. Years later, I handed him a poem about the time he had been jailed for a sit-in protesting racial discrimination and I, being seven in 1964, concluded that he must be dead. He read it and lurched into in my arms, sobbing. I should've kissed him.

Jack Agüeros was my father's compañero and co-conspirator in the Puerto Rican community. Both made images. Many faces lived in my father's camera: a street preacher, a weathered tobacco-picker, a woman grieving the loss of two sons to gang warfare. Jack's sonnets praised a one-legged bicycle messenger, a loquacious character on the unemployment line, the dancers who died in a nightclub fire.

He was the first poet I ever met. Over the years, Jack became my second father. Somewhere, there is a handwritten contract on a paper napkin that says so. I would call whenever I came to New York, and hear: *Agüeros advises declarative sentences—after the beep.* Two generations of Espadas slept on his couch. I would open my eyes to a stack of poems on the table.

We gave readings together. Jack would show up early to defy the stereotype of *PR Time.* He wore a suit, so I wore a suit. He answered a question about why he sometimes wrote in Spanish by saying: *To bust chops!* He was always the quickest guy in the room.

I did not invite Jack to speak at my father's memorial. The quickest guy in the room was dying of Alzheimer's disease. His daughter Natalia called: *If you want to see him, come now.*

I leaned over the rails of Jack's bed to read a poem in his ear, his own "Psalm for Distribution." I smoothed back his hair and kissed his forehead. The hospice nurse said: *Él te conoce.* He knows you.

Jack Agüeros died on May 4, 2014. Two weeks later, Natalia walked to the podium at my father's memorial. She read the words I said to Jack before I kissed him:

Lord,
on 8th Street
between 6th Avenue and Broadway
there are enough shoe stores
with enough shoes
to make me wonder
why there are shoeless people
on the earth.

Lord,
You have to fire the Angel
in charge of distribution.

LEANING IN

Dinty W. Moore

was lucky to see my father once or twice a week, though we lived under the same roof for the first ten years of my life. He had a drinking problem, of the stumble-about, fall-down variety, yet—amazing to me now—he somehow managed to hold down a steady job throughout it all.

What this meant practically was that before I rose for school, my father would be up and out of the house, heading to Dailey's Chevrolet, where he stood in a pit and worked on the undersides of cars. His day ended around four-thirty p.m., but instead of heading home like his fellow mechanics, he would stop at the Cascade Club, drink a bit, play cards. He might stay at the club all evening, or he might drop by Mentley's, or Barilla's, or some other neighborhood bar, for a nightcap.

But just as he always somehow made it to work, Dad was reliable about coming home—staggering in around ten p.m., when I was either fast asleep or just barely awake, listening to the slam of the back door, his unsteady feet on the steps, my mother's voice telling him to stop, that she was sleeping. "No, Bud," she would say. "Not tonight."

To put it plainly, I barely knew my dad, though he was sweet and funny those rare times we did interact, on a Sunday morning before he snuck off for his euchre game, maybe, or on a holiday like Christmas or Easter when the extended family would gather at his sister Grace's house. I saw him more at *her* dining room table than I did at our own.

Around the time I turned ten, my mother left my father, took us away to an apartment, and eventually Dad somehow sobered up. I was too young at the time to understand how difficult that must have been for him, but suddenly I was with my father for hours at a time, having dinner in the room he rented in a sad boardinghouse, then eventually spending entire weekends in the mobile home he purchased, and, in the summer, paddling around the Presque Isle Bay in his canoe.

In my memory, my father never once tucked me in, never once kissed me good night during my childhood. In this new phase, it took a while until we even hugged. He was my father, but a stranger, and neither of us knew exactly how to proceed.

And then one day—I was sixteen, maybe—as we said goodbye near his front doorway, I stretched up on my toes and kissed him, on his unshaven face, on the stubble of his cheek. I can feel it still, the sharpness of the whiskers, the surprisingly soft skin underneath. I can feel, also, him not pulling back, but leaning in.

He didn't live many years longer. I'm sure I kissed him a few more times.

But that first kiss.

I miss him, my dad.

So damn much.

THE REVOLUTIONARY KISS

Tina Chang

had never created man before so I invented my son first as a dream body. In order to create the dream body I must first believe in the force of opposites, a terrible tension of what has existed and the struggle yet to come. And it is true, that I had a notion of him for many years; for generations my imagination traveled in search of him.

It seems unlikely that a kiss would have roots in the Haitian Revolution, but it does. Over a century ago, an uprising of hundreds of thousands of slaves freed themselves from chain and rope, from whip and guillotine, from bondage through the struggle of blood. They fought for thirteen years in a revolution to stand on the shores of their own land, newly named Haiti, as free people, and they kissed the ground however damp with the blood of their mothers, fathers, brothers, and sons. Slaves, newly liberated whispered my son's name, his dream body envisioned there, beneath the rust of shackles, beside shards of slave owners' homes, rising with smoke from burned plantations. Past the pinnacle of scoured light, past the canopy of trees dripping with the uprising of future leaves, my son begins his journey to me.

Once there was a chain of kisses as my mother said goodbye to her brothers and sisters lined in a row, as she left Taiwan for America, a shock of leis around her neck as she waved to a country of ghosts. My mother's history was equally complex. She left China in 1949, when Communists led by Chairman Mao took over mainland China. My mother crowded into a boat that would take her to the coast of Taiwan known as *the beautiful island*, which she would one day yearn to leave.

By foot, by boat, by train, by bus, by plane. It seems impossible these two histories intertwine so that one day I may find a dream body housed inside mine. All along, I wring my hands and worry, will I know how to mother him? What language will I speak? What will my mother utter once she discovers the detour of my ancestry? Will she abandon me, turn the portraits of my ancestors toward the wall, backs directed away from my longing?

When I woke, the doctor's voice was muffled and thick. My mind moved in syncopated pulses and I pushed until all energy drained and my body cracked open. Liquid gold rushed away. Finally and now. He arrived, a purpled creature, violet and squirming, face crushed into an emperor's expression.

Born from the urgency of immigrants, how futile all of my years of worrying. I should have known my boy would row his small boat to me, regardless of the sky above that shook down its lightning, and even if the ground was bruised and famished of fruit and even freedom, he would continue on as if a force were lulling him to bedrock. Right here between his eyebrows, there is swell of light, a country where I belong, no longer a stranger to my own skin. My mouth to his temple, I hear a siren wail from afar and it reminds me the city is a living creature, panting. Tanks roll through the tale squeaking, turning their heavy wheels. I walk inward, over the leaves, and they illuminate. I know there is a will beyond me. I am ready now to hold the weight of my son. When I kiss him, history's weapons fall from my pockets, shields cast beneath attalea trees. I will now end my days of resistance, my lips searching the entirety of his dream face made mortal, my lost shadows now migrating in unison.

THE HEAVY LOAD

Adam Dalva

My OCD (and we're talking diagnosis, not topic-sentence short-hand for fussy) tends to manifest harmlessly. I like to count bottles above bars until the one on the top-right matches my age; at thirty-one, this is proving quite difficult. I take an occasional Klonopin to sleep if I can't stop picturing, say, the lesser Greek gods frolicking in vivid 3-D above my bed for hours. Lately, I fear that I'm going to throw a glass of water in someone's face, so I spend restaurant meals clutching tablecloths and suffering through awkward ideations that feel more real than reality. These things pass. But a pernicious, decade-long symptom is my desire—no, my need—to be kissed on New Year's Eve at midnight.

Since my first kiss, age eighteen, I have never not kissed someone at that terminal moment of New Year's Eve, as everyone shouts and gesticulates. My first year after college, I spent the holiday in an abysmal pirate-themed bar on Manhattan's Upper West Side. Despite the entreaties of the paid "galley wenches," I was reading a book, miserable, when a woman approached me. Let's call her Amanda, since her name was Amanda. "I want to eat your brain," Amanda said, tapping my Salinger, and as 2009 hit, we were smooching. The next year, I went back to the same horrible bar with the same horrible friends, and again, I was approached, and I should clarify here that though I really am quite nice, I'm not the sort who's approached for a spontaneous kiss very often.

By November of 2010, I'd started to wonder if it was going to happen again. This strain of narrative curiosity is the root of my OCD. Wonder becomes hope becomes the need to enact, and so with fifteen minutes to go on David Zee's West Village roof above an anodyne sex shop, I was considering a gallant offer from my friend Matt, who is gay, who is a man.

I did not want to kiss Matt—not only am I not attracted to men, but he was also my best friend's ex-boyfriend, and my best friend is the type who will cut you out for less. Still: the compulsion. Matt and I made out for a bit. God, it was horrible—mechanical and aloof and scratchy and the way his tongue ran between the groove in my front teeth was sort of hypothetically sexy until I confronted the reality that it was Matt, that my best friend had been greatly moved by this sensation, that several people on the roof were thoroughly confused, that my disgust said something damning about my flatlining Kinsey scale. "That's so cool," various women have since exclaimed when they ask if I've been physical with a man, and I don't know how to tell them that, even beyond their disappointing alignment of coolness with sexual preference, there was nothing cool about it.

The next year, I had just started dating someone new, and it became clear that she was going to be late to the New Year's party. There had been no discussion of monogamy and I felt as I always do when OCD begins to set in—it's a crawling need, a buzz that must be stopped. Teeth clench; toes wiggle. I was approached around eleven p.m., which felt like inevitability. Never mind that the approacher had a strange affect. Her dress was made of sparkles; her wig was voluminous; she was a woman. I agreed to our midnight rendezvous.

The party was at one of those Williamsburg apartment complexes where no one knows the owner, though one presumes he's in the most obnoxious quadrant of the party, and there were multiple balconies. I went to the top one, intentionally separate from my friends. It's quite warm out in memory, but perhaps it just wasn't notably cold. I stood there alone. Honestly, I was sort of hoping that my appointment wouldn't find me. Maybe things could be different in 2012. But she arrived. There were going to be fireworks that year, and as everyone began counting down, I turned and looked toward the East River, metallic and distant and fine. Hundreds of thousands of people before me, most counting, many about to kiss. Things felt tenuous, and I saw that she was looking up at me, still sparkly, lips pursed, leaning in as three and two were shouted by all, as our four eyelashes fluttered.

It's nearing, as we approach T-0, the time for me to describe the kiss. And this would usually present a problem: I've never been good at that. I once described lips in my novel as warm and soft, and Lorrie Moore, in the midst of her only workshop in NYU, Lorrie Moore who is a hero of mine, said, "Lips are never warm and soft, Adam." Barely concealed disdain flashed across her face. "They are *only* ever chapped and spicy." It was a perfect Lorrie Moore two-set. I laughed and nodded and felt like vomiting, but I've never figured out my own chapped and spicy. All my kisses have been warm and soft, with the exception of Matt, which was like kissing two re-animating worms stuck to hot concrete.

Regardless, it was time to kiss this woman I didn't want to kiss. At first it was warm, and soft, and wet. Fireworks went off. People were cheering. I felt very, very observed. And then an object passed from her mouth into mine. A tooth, small and hard. No, two teeth. I unlocked and spat the objects out onto the thronged balcony below, then turned back to see her smiling at me. I looked down at her hand. Reader, she was holding a raisin box. The little Sun-Maid one, red, with the blushing lady presenting the grapes and the hot sun pounding down. She had passed two rehydrated raisins from her mouth into mine. The woman nodded at me, then vanished forever.

Me? I'm a tinkerer of my own past. But this is the only event in my life that remains completely, frustratingly opaque. It must have been intentional—it was a New Year's kiss, the one kiss a year that's totally planned, when we count down, when there are cues. And she had asked to kiss me. We've all successfully kissed with chewing gum in our mouths without said gum crossing the Rubicon; she must have planned it. But why? No one saw it happen, barely anyone believes me. Maybe it was a fetish—maybe it was her own compulsion.

Finally, the woman I ended up dating arrived, and we kissed on the subway platform on the way home. She never found out about the incident. I've told very few people about it since. I should make clear that this isn't a story about getting better. They rarely are for me. Every year since, I've kissed someone at midnight. I have broken up with two different women at New Years' parties, one at two a.m., the other at four, but each year, I've managed to stop the buzz. And every time I do now, there is the remembered ghost of raisins, sweet and just a bit wet (which, now that I write it, is a half-decent description of a kiss).

MAUDE

Kimiko Hahn

What would her lips feel *like*—? *A tulip petal? A porcelain bowl?*

The last time I saw her, she was waving goodbye as Ted and I drove off with the baby, already snoozing in the backseat. I saw her turn away to climb the three dozen steps back to the shambly house. Not her fault, the shambles. Not the fault of mice or the snow that settled into a crust on the flat roof.

Days later, Father took her to the Kabuki. On the drive home, a car of teenagers broadsided them. Father cursed. Mother lay slumped on the passenger side. He didn't realize she was dead.

A metal bowl? Doily? Birch bark? Page torn from an old book?

Ted and I decided to see her at the funeral home. To "view her" in the pine coffin. Before she was delivered to the crematorium. The undertaker commented on how "Orientals don't show their age." Sixty-eight, only a few years older than I am today. I looked. But I didn't clip a wisp of hair as keepsake. I didn't touch her clothes or her hand. It was enough to see what I would come to describe as *the body that was Mother's.*

Ice? I was told not to put lips or tongue on ice because my skin would stick fast.

Was I afraid to kiss her on the lips or did that sense just occur to me? Afraid to kiss the lips that were my mother's? *Pumice? Bar of soap? Like* both connects and keeps at arm's length.

(Had she wanted to go?)

JUDAS KISS

Tom Sleigh

When I asked a friend what I should write about, she said, "There's always a betrayal in a kiss." I won't belabor the point, since I'm sure you can work it out on your own—but I immediately thought of Judas kissing Jesus in order to show the Jewish council's soldiers whom they should arrest. There's a painting by Giotto in which Judas wraps his long, flowing silver robe around Jesus, engulfing him as he moves in for the kill, much the way Bela Lugosi in his long cape moves in on his victims in the old Dracula movies. And like Dracula, there's a look of almost helpless resignation and, even worse, self-recognition in Judas's eyes that lets you know that he knows he's a monster.

Anyone over the age of fifty knows that look; by that time of life, who hasn't betrayed or been betrayed by a lover, parent, or a friend? The kiss I gave to my dying father was a kiss of betrayal for not going down to the grave with him. And when I was shooting dope at sixteen, and he searched my pockets where I'd carelessly left my fix, and confronted me about the baggie of heroin, I felt violated by him for going through my pockets without asking. I try to snatch the baggie out of his hand, we scuffle, he somehow manages to flush it down the toilet. *This is hard drugs!* he shouts. *You shouldn't steal stuff from my pockets!* I shout back. And then my father tries to kiss me: but I shrink back from him even as our eyes lock—and then he touches me gently on the shoulder as if his touch could fix what is unfixable.

But this moment of private pathos isn't my only focus here. There's a short story by Borges in which he speculates that God actually incarnated himself in Judas, not Jesus. He says that Judas made the ultimate sacrifice by ensuring his own damnation and eternal revilement. When Judas takes the thirty pieces of silver, when he kisses Jesus in the Garden of Gethsemane just after Jesus, in an agony of fear about being nailed to the cross, has prayed to his Father to allow the cup to pass, when the soldiers seize Jesus and take him before Caiaphas the high priest, when Judas in despair then hangs himself—what greater sacrifice could there be? Traitor, suicide, sell-out. But Judas knew his fate was foretold from the world's beginning. And in the bitterness of that fate, not only did he know that the magnitude of his sacrifice would go misunderstood, he knew it would never be recognized.

And he did this for us, so that none of us would ever have to feel alone in such depths of degradation and depravity.

Unlike Judas, whose hateful act becomes in our sinful eyes an act of love, in a Benetton ad campaign five years ago, world leaders who are archenemies are Photoshopped to look as if they are kissing each other on the mouth: the UNHATE ad campaign. Obama kisses Hu Jintao of China, Mahmoud Abbas of Palestine kisses Benjamin Netanyahu of Israel, Kim Jong-il of North Korea kisses Lee Myung-bak of

South Korea, and so on. What all these leaders have in common as they smooch is that their eyes are closed: these seem like erotic kisses, not formal ones. Only Jesus and Judas have their eyes wide open, as if they knew their kiss would be a source of eternal bitterness to the other. These bromances are comic and creepy and wonderfully upsetting of hetero respectability—maybe an orgy at the UN would be in order?

And then there's Donald Trump—kissing various Ms. Universes, kissing Melania, kissing babies and children, including a little African-American girl who turns her head away, air-kissing Mike Pence who wears an embarassed smile and also turns away; and in an image lampooning them both, Trump and Ted Cruz puckering up on a billboard promoting an end to homophobia.

But kissing is far from universal: in fact, less than half of the world's cultures kiss for romantic purposes, and almost no animals. I think of my father's helpless attempt to kiss his wayward child, and of Trump and Jesus and Judas and the world leaders, and rather than words comes the image of a sea lion and its trainer. The trainer holds a fish in one hand and when the sea lion pecks his cheek, he throws a fish to the sea lion, who gulps it down and claps its flippers. This kiss is also a Judas kiss, an act of intraspecies betrayal: the man wants the sea lion to act like a man, but all it can do is act like a sea lion trained to act like a man. And for the sea lion's part, the kiss means nothing but a fish. Now, supported by the man who wraps one arm around it, the sea lion galumphs up on its hind flippers. Locked in a clumsy embrace, the sea lion gapes its mouth open so wide that it almost swallows the whole head of the man.

THE SMUGGLER

Ada Limón

t's been a whole month since I've seen you, so I've taken to talking to you while I do simple things around the house. It's a drowsy sort of madness. To lighten the mood (the one I get in, you know, all ink and plummet), I bought the brightest yellow tulips I could find and placed them on our huge vintage coffee table that anchors our bodies when we're home. Distance is a strange dissection of the mind. I live in two places. Where I am and where you are. This morning, I woke up and thought I was in that shitty cabin in Ocala with you, but instead I was in a well-lit home in Kentucky, the dog's rough paw over my mouth, as if blocking me from speaking. I dreamt of tsunamis and tidal waves coming to wash everything clean.

On the morning walk today, I saw a hospice nurse leaving our neighbor's house, the brick one across the street, two doors down. She must be visiting the woman whose dog you saved in that dark October night when the dog, half blind, wandered into traffic. I wonder if that ancient dog's all right. She had one foot on the train tracks. Our neigh-bor called the dog Little Guy, but she was a girl. She bit you with what was left of her teeth and you didn't even care, praised her for trying, even, and gathered her surrendered body in your arms and carried her home. Anyway, I knew the visitor was a hospice nurse because of what she carried, and how she kept her head down, like a wise dog knowing exactly where the weaving trail leads.

Our dog is snoring right now as I write this. Spoiled and content. Swaddled in gray blankets like the hazy sun swirled in fog. Sometimes I think everything we do is formed by death. You wrote me right after C died, though you and I had already made out hard once at a holiday party, mouths thirsty for each other, all the colored lights blurring in the periphery and the dirty smog of winter smoke in the air. After C's memorial, after the hospice nurse had left, and T pulled all the wine away from the guests, T and I slept in the white guest room upstairs. I checked my email in the morning. There were your words, so bare on the gray screen, and all in lowercase like you were bowing to the grief I was thrown into. When T woke up, her hair wild around her shoulders, she said she had the most vivid dream that I was walking in the North-west woods and a blue plaid bird landed on my shoulder. Sometimes we still call you that plaid bird.

And now, nearly seven years later, your ex has died, the gorgeous girl right before it was my turn to love you, and there's more grief we bow and bend toward. I was in Texas when you told me. I sobbed in the giant bathtub, for you and for her, and for her and then for you again, then again for me, selfish as I am, always for me. I don't know if I've told you this, but what I remember most was the second kiss. The one after the death was nearly three months behind me and we sat in the back-yard of that Italian place off Metropolitan and Bushwick. The place was called Il Passatore, which later I found out meant "The Smuggler" in Italian. You leaned in to kiss me outside on the spring sidewalk among Brooklyn's many broken tulips, petals all tipsy from traffic, and I felt like I could breathe again. Like it was not a kiss, but a resuscitation. I was smuggled back into the world again, under your arm like that foggy-eyed dog you saved from the oncoming cars.

I can hear the train going by now. I love the sound it makes, singular and straightforward, not like life at all. The sun's coming out stronger and I'll see you again in three days. And in two months we'll be married on the mountaintop. I think of all the footprints we'll carry with us in our heads, the dead moving through us like air, how each touch seems to be a reminder of what we cannot touch again. All this to say, thank you, I love what your mouth does to me: how it reminds me where I am and what I'm doing, how in kissing you I'm kissing all those who kissed you and you're kissing all those who kissed me, this breath we pass to each other is proof that we're still living.

A KISS FOR THE DYING

Suzanne Roberts

1.

Mother has been told that she is dying. Maybe three months, the internist says with a shrug. He listens to her heart, the lungs filled with tumors. Then he says, "What you have is very bad."

Mother pulls a face at him. I try not to laugh.

When the pulmonologist walks into the room, Mother asks, "Have you heard? I'm a goner."

He doesn't answer her, and he takes her pulse. "It's very fast," he says, and then tells her that there's a nerve on her neck, that if he presses on it, the heart will slow down.

It works, and Mother says, "You should go to Vegas," meaning that he might take his magic trick on the road. But he only hears "vagus," and he says, "Very good! That *is* your vagus nerve."

We all laugh, except the doctor, who is very serious.

2.

For the past few months, Mother had lost her sense of humor, and when I asked her why, she said, "Because nothing is funny anymore." She hadn't been feeling well, thought it was her heart, wondered why she wasn't getting any better. But once she was diagnosed with extensive small cell lung cancer, the most aggressive form of lung cancer, everything is funny again, even things that aren't. Like the man in the hospital room next door, wailing to anyone who passes his room, "Nurse, help me. Nurse? Doctor? Help me."

Mother is getting a blood transfusion, and by the second bag of blood, Mother starts imitating him: *Nurse! Help me!* The only thing that saves this from being mean is that he is constipated, and she's dying. So it only seems fair. Even our nurse, who has tired of this man's constant moaning, laughs with us.

When I leave her room, I walk to the side of her hospital bed, and I bend down under the fluorescent lights to kiss her. The skin on her forehead is sometimes dry and papery beneath my lips, sometimes it is cold and damp. I kiss her, and I say the same thing, every time. I say, "Don't die, okay?"

And she says, "No, I won't." And we laugh.

3.

I ask Mother if she remembers her first kiss with my father. She laughs and says, "Of course I do."

"Tell me."

"Well," she says. "It was after our first date. We went to the beach, and when he dropped me off, he kissed me."

"Did he ask you first?"

"No, but he knew."

"How?"

"A woman has a way of showing it. You should know," she says. "But more than that first kiss. I knew I wanted to marry him the minute I met him. It's strange to me now. But I just knew."

4.

Mother asks me if I remember my first kiss.

I tell her the oleander rustled in the hot Santa Ana winds, and the asphalt melted beneath my Keds. Then his tongue entered my mouth like a surprise. I could not have pictured that development when I kissed my pillow, practicing for the moment. I didn't know that slipping a tongue into another's mouth was a thing. I had heard of French kissing and thought it meant tilting your head and kissing for a long time. Or a kind of kissing invented in France—something foreign and mysterious. I wasn't sure, but I wouldn't have guessed it involved the tongue.

I didn't know that, within a few days, this boy would tell me it was over. Or that this first kiss, and the kisses that followed, would do nothing to save me from the horrors of junior high school. And that after this first kiss, everything else would come far too quickly.

I knew only that the kiss tasted like Jolly Rancher sour apple candy and that everything else disappeared—my eyes shut tight to the afternoon sun of my own becoming.

5.

I ask Mother to tell me about the first time she kissed me.

"It wasn't right away. They took you away and cleaned you. I couldn't wait for the nurses to bring you back, and when they did, I kissed you."

"Where?" I ask, but I already know the answer.

"On the forehead. And your father did, too. And you had this blue vein that sort of popped out there. Your father was so worried about it. But I knew it would be fine, and it was."

There are pictures around her house of Mother and me when I am little, and in some, we are kissing. There are no such pictures of me and my father. I do not remember ever kissing him, and I wasn't there when he died, so I never kissed him goodbye.

Sometimes he comes back to me in dreams, but by the time I reach him, he's already gone.

On my way out of Mother's hospital room, I rub foamy hand sanitizer into my hands, a ritual that has come to feel something like prayer. And next door, the howling, and the smell of blood and urine, disinfectant and shit. I walk the shiny halls and then come back to her room and leave again, and every time I go, I say it: I kiss her goodbye on the forehead, and I say, *Don't die*, and she doesn't.

It's only funny if she stays alive.

MAN WITHOUT FEAR

Sholeh Wolpé

When I was on the island of San Simón, I fell in love with a stone man.

Besides him, there were nine of us: seven poets, a cook, and a boatman. The poets came to this northern Spanish island to commune and translate one another's poems. The cook fed us and the boatman ferried us to the mainland as needed.

The island's history was heavy. Franco sent his enemies here to be executed. First a prison, the island then became a military garrison, and finally a place for the incurable, the hopeless, and the mentally ill.

Now it was a place for governmental use. For special guests. And so, for one week, we were those special people. The poets. Each from a different corner of the world.

Every day we took a break in the afternoon, and while the others wrote, bathed, or napped, I explored the tiny island, so small that it took only fifteen minutes to walk its shores from one end to the other.

Franco carried out his executions beyond the bridge where we stayed. A sign said this was the priests' section. As I walked toward the extreme end of the island, I reached a wall against which Franco shot men. Behind it was a roofless room with rock walls and five unmarked graves of various sizes. Next to that was a large enclosure in which the stone man stood. We were chin to chin if I stood on my tiptoes. *Hombre sin miedo*, the man without fear, facing the water. When I entered the enclosure, the air changed color.

He had been waiting. Eyes carved wide, full lips, arms folded, hands twice the size of mine, he was deprived of feet. Was it because the artist ran out of patience or time? Did he fear that his creation might one day unroot and walk into the sea? Why did he name him the man without fear?

I visited this section every day. First the buried unknowns, for whom I would sing, then my *hombre sin miedo*, with whom I spoke. He was a good listener. And I had so much to confess. But I will not tell it here. Some sins are only for ears made of stone.

I ran my fingers along his deep-carved eyes, his large head, his lichen-covered torso. Who would have thought stone could be so soft, so sensual? To love a man made of stone is no different from loving a poet long dead. It's mostly the presence that you love. The heart is not always drawn to what is made of flesh. Isn't the body a vehicle for the soul? Who's to say that the duende of my *hombre sin miedo* was not tied to a spirit behind that wall?

I put my lips on his. The breeze shivered. The ghosts next door watched us from among the tree branches. The water's music shifted to a lower key. The birds hovered. And as I closed my eyes, a draft of air lifted my red scarf and wrapped it around his thick stony neck. My *hombre sin miedo*.

WINTER SOLSTICE

Bich Minh Nguyen

n my family, people didn't kiss. My parents never kissed my siblings and me good night. They didn't kiss each other in front of us. If a couple started kissing on a TV show, they changed the channel. There was certainly none of that kissing on the cheek as a greeting. We didn't even hug.

This was the 1980s in Michigan and we were Vietnamese refugees. We were always trying to figure out white Americans and how we were supposed to behave. Except my grandmother Noi. She didn't worry about things like that. She had raised four children on her own and uprooted her life twice, from Hanoi to Saigon and then to the United States. I knew her as the matriarch, the one who could not be messed with when it came to cooking, knitting, orchid-growing, or just *being*. She was a calm, no-nonsense figure, and I was hardly ever happier than when we were eating ramen together and watching her favorite American soap operas.

I never kissed my grandmother Noi. She never kissed me. Maybe it was an Asian thing; maybe it was our family. I knew she loved me and she knew I loved her, yet we never said it. Not in any language. Instead we ate fruit and laughed at sitcoms and wondered who would marry whom on *Santa Barbara*. At night I would jokingly ask her if it was okay to go to sleep and she would say yes, it's okay.

Noi died in 2007, on the winter solstice. I drove from Chicago, where I was living then, to Grand Rapids, Michigan, to the hospital where she had been taken after she collapsed. An aortic dissection, it would turn out. It was the only time she had ever been admitted to a hospital, and by then she was already dead.

It snowed hard the next couple of days. My grandmother's body, by Buddhist tradition, lay in an open coffin in my parents' house. Guests came by to pay their respects and we wore white cloths around our heads. The night before we drove her body to the crematory, I kept wanting to see her one more time. She was dressed in a silver ao dai, one that she had made herself, and her silver hair was in its usual bun. She was eighty-seven years old. The last time I had seen her alive, she had stood on her tiptoes to water a hanging plant in her living room. Now her body would become ash, though it was already something or somewhere or someone else, unknowable.

How many nights, growing up, had I walked around sleeplessly only to find that my grandmother was also awake, waiting for me?

I touched her wrist. I kissed my grandmother Noi. Her forehead, her cheek. I do not mean to say that it was necessary. It wasn't. We were not ones to say I love you. Our language never needed that. And I have never written this, or told anyone this, until now. The kiss, I knew even then, was more for me than for her. She would have understood that. She would have understood all of this.

THE GREATEST SHOW ON EARTH

KRISTEN RADTKE

There was this circus that set up in the middle of the state for a few weeks every summer when I was a kid. That was before we knew circuses were bad, or maybe people knew somewhere, but in our splintered, worn-down northern Wisconsin town, no one ever thought about it.

The circus was small, a little tent in the center of a field, but of course we didn't know it was small, we didn't know there were bigger circuses in other places. We didn't even know there were other places.

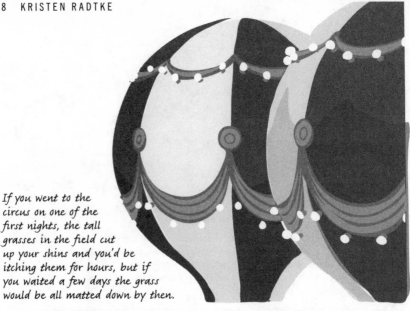

If you went to the circus on one of the first nights, the tall grasses in the field cut up your shins and you'd be itching them for hours, but if you waited a few days the grass would be all matted down by then.

All night, every night, the ringmaster announced between acts that at the end of the show he'd bring out a monkey, and it would be the tiniest, the cutest monkey in the world. And if the monkey kissed any one of us, that person would get a prize. We all wanted that prize. It was something really good, like candy, like a toy, like money.

When the ringmaster finally brought the monkey out we saw that it was true: he was the tiniest, the cutest monkey we had ever seen. He wrapped his legs around the ring-master's side like he was a toddler and the ring-master was his mother, the monkey's arms wrapped around the ring-master's neck, his head craning toward the audience.

Up close the ringmaster's face was bad, scrunched and pulled like he was smelling something rotten or like he was something rotten. When I saw his face I didn't want to be at the front of the crowd anymore.

The monkey knew he was supposed to kiss the people, I could
tell that he'd been trained for
it, the way he swung his body
toward us. But I could see how
tight the man's fingers were
digging into the monkey's back.
    The man walked the
perimeter of the ring quickly,
and a few inches too far from
the edge of the crowd, so no
matter how hard the monkey
pushed his tiny body forward,
he couldn't reach the people.

The whole audience was crazed trying to
get the monkey to kiss them. They
reached their arms out and pushed their
elbows into each other's sides and wedged
their legs between any gaps they could
find to pull themselves closer.

It was like we weren't people anymore, crammed in so tightly in that tent on
the dirt circus floor, and it was like the ringmaster knew it. He looked at us
like we weren't people and I knew it, too.

SKEERY THE BLUE

Christian Kiefer

My father's name was Colgate, a name which, like my own and that of my brother, meant something in the forgotten world before this one but which, now, today, is but a name like any other. I had lost my mother when I was young, so my father had been, in effect, both of my parents in one. It was he who conferenced with my teachers, he who patched me up when I was hurt, he who fed and clothed me, and he, too, who suffered my anger and scorn when things did not go my way. So when he died abruptly soon after my fifteenth birthday, I felt as if my whole world—everything I knew or expected or counted on—had vanished into black empty space. In the days to follow, I simply could not believe that he was gone, still turning toward his absence when I found an interesting snippet of text, an equation worth discussing, a piece of vocabulary from some language he had mastered but I was just learning. But that chair, the chair in which he sat in the evenings, watching the screens and sipping cognac, was empty and would always be empty no matter how many times I turned to its soft, padded surfaces.

My brother Victrola and I were separated by seven years and, as such, lived separate lives, I with my father in our family apartment and my brother across the outpost in the warren of inexpensive housing known simply as "the Quay," a collection of boxy dwellings stacked one upon the other until they appeared as if toppling rows of tall, thin bookshelves, the tiny apartments there occupied by the outpost's work-ing class, would-be writers and artists, drug addicts, immigrants, and, like my brother, students living on the cheap. It was, to me, a frantic and beautiful chaos, its colors and textures and sounds and smells a confusion of acrid beauty and florid decay that sent my head spinning to catch hold of it all.

After my father's death, what I wished for—and indeed what I assumed would occur—was for Victrola to move back home. But alas the apartment had been rented from the housing works and, with-out regular payments, payments neither I nor my brother could make despite the small cash settlement we had received from my father's will, the space was offered to a new renter and I, a fifteen-year-old girl with little knowledge of the world outside of school and homework and the various screens I consulted for entertainment and communication, was summarily evicted from the only home I had ever known. What remained were two suitcases carried by my brother and containing all my worldly belongings: my screens, my clothing, a photograph of myself with my brother and father, and a few small odds and ends that I had kept as mementos of my former life.

I did not question my brother's willingness to take me in and indeed my sadness was slightly lessened by the fact that I was, at least, still among family, still taken care of. I thought I knew him, of course—

after all, he was my brother—and yet it was not until I actually arrived at his apartment to stay that I truly understood just how separate Victrola's life had become from that of myself and our father, separate and, as I was to learn, quite private, for while I knew my brother to have had various girlfriends at one time or another, some of whom he had even brought by the apartment to introduce to our father and, to a lesser extent, to me, the fact that he had a girlfriend now, and the further complication that she lived with him in his apartment—a much smaller, much tighter space than I was accustomed to—had not occurred to me even as a remote possibility. The first indication of my own ignorance came immediately upon arriving at his door, when, instead of opening it, Victrola remained outside for a long, strange moment, his head slightly tilted as if listening for some sound or signal from within.

"What are you doing?" I asked him. "Aren't we going in?"

He had already straightened, nodding as if nothing were amiss at all, but when the door slid open with its thin, reedy swish, I saw immediately that something significant had, indeed, changed, at least for me. There, in the center of the room, stood, in utter silence, a tall luminous figure wrapped in a pale shift, her skin's tiny grained channels coursing with slowly pulsing light.

It is a bizarre admission in the wake of all that happened, but Skeery was the first Blue I ever met. Of course I had seen them and, in my sentient biology classes, had studied their physiological differences from humans, but I had never had any meaningful interaction with a member of that species. My only experience with their system of telepathic communication had come in a classroom when a Blue, the guest of the professor, had sent a brief message to the assembled students: phrases and a scattering of related images. The reaction of the students had been, unilaterally, to gasp in alarm, a reaction I was to repeat as my brother's live-in girlfriend—for that is what she was—brushed her message across my mind.

"Hedge," my brother said softly, "this is Skeery."

The feeling—in the classroom and in my brother's apartment—was like the briefest tickle under the flesh of my forehead and then, a fraction of a second later, a blooming of words and images. *You Hedgerow Greeting Happy*, Skeery said into my frontal lobe, the individual words popping like bubbles, behind which, in a brief flash, came the image of a purple hill with a blazing white sun hovering just above, its light so bright that it felt, for that briefest flicker, as if I were being blinded from the inside. I must have made some kind of sound, for my brother's hand was on my shoulder now, my mind still ringing from the flash of light. "It's a common greeting," he said. "It's meant to make you feel at ease."

I may have said something in reply, but really I could do little more than stare at the creature before me. Skeery was, at least to me, at least then, indistinguishable from any other of her species, close enough to the shape of a human to create within me a central revulsion that embarrassed me and which I could not control. Her head was mostly shaped like a human head, although slightly larger, and of course her skin was the pale, almost luminescent blue that had given the species their common nickname. Her eyes roughly coincided with the location of human eyes, although Skeery's (like all Blues) were large, without pupils, vaguely larval in appearance, their color the yellow of old teeth. But what disturbed me most was not the expressionless ovoid eyes or the hue of Skeery's skin but the fact that the area just below her nose slipped, at a fairly regular angle, into her neck, unbroken by mouth, jaw, or chin, so that her entire head, especially in profile, had the oblong shape of a balloon.

"Hello," I said quietly.

The tickle again. *You Hedgerow Greeting*, she said to my mind. A flicker of the hill, the blazing sun.

"That's really bright," I said absently.

You Hedgerow Smile.

I did not know if she meant that I made her smile or if she was asking or even commanding me to smile, but then an image of Skeery herself came, with a smile drawn upon her mouthless face as if with an ink-soaked brush, the effect so strange, so disconcerting, that I actually burst into a laugh.

Skeery stepped forward now and reached out her hand, and after a moment I took it, the feeling warm and so soft it almost felt as if I held something made entirely of water, as if I could crush it between my fingers.

You Hedgerow Meeting Good.

"It's . . . uh . . . nice to meet you, too," I said falteringly.

"She's your girlfriend? Your *girlfriend*?"

"She is," my brother said.

There was no food in the apartment—a fact I could hardly understand at the time—and Victrola and I had gone out for ramen, the bowls hot, the liquid steaming my face as I ate. Had it been a few weeks earlier I might have reveled in the experience—eating from a street cart in the Quay, the flavors and smells in the air all around me—but in the face of what I had learned about my brother and about the living situation in which I had now found myself, I could hardly taste the meal at all.

"How long?"

"Have we been seeing each other? Two quarters, I guess."

"Two quarters," I repeated.

"I'm surprised you're so shocked," he said then. "I thought you'd be more open-minded."

"I am open-minded," I said. And yet I had already come to realize that this statement might not have been quite so true as I thought. From the street outside, through the grimy windows, came the churning motion of the pedestrians and peddlers and hawkers of the Quay, some human, some Blue, some the scattered members of other sentient species.

"Just give her a chance, Hedge," my brother told me gently. "She's great. You'll see."

We fell silent for a moment, each of us spooning ramen into our mouths, slurping, chewing. What I thought then was just how much I missed my father, how I wanted, more than anything, to return to the familiar apartment in which I had lived all my life. But my home was gone and the only place I had to turn was to my brother's cramped student quarters which, even now, contained the luminous figure of Skeery, her silent, lidless, insectoid eyes ever-watchful.

"We look pretty weird to them, too, you know," my brother said then, as if he could hear my thoughts.

"She told you that?"

"Not exactly, but I know the idea of eating is pretty primitive to them. And shitting is positively disgusting."

"So what do you do?"

"What we're doing right now," he said. "Eat out."

"Really?"

He smiled, that dazzling arc of shining teeth. "Really," he said. "You can't control what the heart does, Hedge."

"Sure you can," I told him. "You wouldn't let yourself fall in love with a fork or a toaster oven or a glass of water."

"Don't be an ass."

"Well, it's true. You can't even kiss her."

My brother looked at me then, his eyes narrowing. "There's more to a relationship than kissing," he said.

From my point of view, age fifteen and in the throes of my first relationship, my brother's statement was demonstrably untrue. My boyfriend Sim was a year older than I and it was clear almost from the start that my body was not the first female shape he had held in his thin, elegant hands. He was emotional, gentle, beautiful to look at, and even now, so many years later, I feel a pang somewhere deep and secret when I think of those days, not just of him but of he and I together, our youthful passion, the way our first kiss flooded through me like a bloodwave filling me from everywhere at once, our lips touching tentatively at first and then the flick of his tongue across my closed mouth, my teeth, and then nothing but the depths of our hunger. It is this experience—the kissing—that I returned to when I thought of my brother and Skeery, this that I return to even now, the realization of the differences in their physiognomy that meant he would never kiss her, that they would never kiss each other. The very idea of it seemed impossible to me. In those few memories I had of my mother, I could see my father kissing her, his hands holding her. It was, I knew, my blueprint for what a healthy relationship was supposed to be, what it was supposed to look like; even now it is not the sexual act that I think of when I ponder the physical manifestations of human love but instead the warmth of kissing and holding and speaking. Sim told me he loved me. I told him the same. This was what mattered.

So even beyond my own physical reaction to Skeery, I simply wondered what Victrola saw in her. True, there was undeniable beauty in her pale blue skin with its series of finely etched sparkling lines, lines that reminded me of wood grain but which coursed with visible energy like electric wires, and of course there was a certain gracefulness in her motion, an attribute common to the Blue (even watching one of her species walk across a room was like being secret witness to some subtle aquatic ballet), but fundamentally I could not understand looking at that mouthless face with its great yellowish larval eyes and had especial trouble imagining Victrola finding pleasure in that vision. Those of his previous girlfriends I had seen—all human—had been unilaterally beautiful—and quite capable of holding down a reasonably intelligent conversation, one not limited to random flashing words and weird pictures of purple grass and blinding sunlight.

And yet, even then, especially then, it was impossible not to see that my brother was happy during his year with Skeery. Later I would come to wonder if that was the happiest time in his life, since the rest of it—his two marriages, his estranged adult children, the scandals that would periodically rock his personal and public lives—brought to him a depth of sadness that was likely hidden to all but me, his only living family, but in the days of Skeery, when he was but a boy of twenty-two, the whole world before him, he seemed to burn with a bright and luminous fire. Was it Skeery who gave him that? I did not think so at the time but now it seems obvious that it was she who brought out that rare and wondrous quality in my brother, the bright spark of him at twenty-two when he was enthralled by a love that was quite simply beyond my ability to understand.

Of course, there was so much I did not understand then, not only about that relationship but about my brother and about myself, for I had already sowed the seeds that would lead to the end of Skeery's presence in our lives. That I had done so totally unwittingly only serves to underscore how oblivious I was and, perhaps, how oblivious I still am. That I have spent all of my adult life in the presence of the Blue may be a ready metaphor of penance for my sins, but really my decision to live among them has more to do with the mundane aspects of my physical life than it does with anything else. Suffice to say, some character flaws run deeply enough that they cannot be excavated no matter how many hours we spend in the therapist's chair, and I can assure you that I have spent a good many hours spilling my secrets in that context, my mouth silent but my mind filled with the images of my own guilty conscience.

I realize now that she was trying to be my friend, in her way. Perhaps the cultural differences made it impossible for me to understand the cues, or perhaps the physical differences, the differences in actual species, were too great a barrier; in any case I did not reciprocate the attempt. In my defense, my father's sudden death continued to weigh heavy upon my heart. Sometimes at night I wrapped my arms around myself in the darkness of my sleeping mat and imagined that I was a child of six or eight or ten and my father had tucked me into bed and all was right in the world. The arms that encircled me were his arms, as were the little kisses I imagined upon my forehead, my cheeks, my eyes. During such times, I sometimes thought I could feel the faintest tickle somewhere in my forehead, my frontal lobe tingling, but when I focused on that sensation it was just as quickly gone, like something

just at the edge of my vision, an illusion, a dream. Was it Skeery listening to my grief? I did not know and could not think of a way to ask. In
the mornings, after I had cried myself to sleep, I sometimes thought I
could read concern upon her emotionless visage, her great larval eyes
seeming to stare at me from across the room. I said nothing. She said
the same.

We ate every meal out, of course, my brother and I, and I knew,
too, that in our absence from the apartment, Skeery fed upon the light
from the sunpanels. Victrola had shown me the panels soon after I had
arrived at the apartment.

"Don't ever come in here without letting us know," he told me once,
gesturing through the open bedroom door.

"Don't worry about that," I said. "I don't want to walk in on anything."

"It's not that," he said seriously. "Those lights can kill you."

"What do you mean?"

"I mean they can kill you," he said. "It's meant to simulate the sun
on the Blue homeworld. It's three times as bright as ours."

"Why doesn't she just go out to eat?"

"She could," he said, "but the closest public sunpanels are across
base in Loomtown."

The panels were matte-black when powered down, so dark, in fact,
that it was difficult to imagine them emitting light of any kind. That
something like this was here, in my brother's bedroom, in this tiny
apartment, felt like being shown that a bomb was set just a few feet
from where, each night, Victrola slept side by side with a female of a
different species. The very thought made my heart leap with an agony
of fear.

"It's a lot to take in," my brother said then. "Just give it some time."

I wish I could say that I followed my brother's advice, that I did, indeed, "give it some time," but the reality was that I dealt with the situation, with the cohabitation, by avoiding her entirely. I tried, during the next two quarters, to spend as much time as possible at school or with Sim, but even beyond such measures of physical separation, I simply avoided interacting with her at all, thinking of her as some vaguely humanoid pet that my brother had somehow trained to follow him around, a creature who sat in total silence, only on rare occasions communicating something to me in passing, the common words and phrases sounding forced and awkward in my thoughts as if I were picking up a hazy broadcast from a language school.

You Hedgerow Say Thing Funny Victrola.

You Hedgerow Want Glass Water.

You Hedgerow Tired Eyes Sleep Look.

You Hedgerow Day Bright Sun.

Often the sentences were accompanied by a quick flicker of imagery: the quad at school in the summer sun; a bed, soft pillow awaiting my head; a clear shining glass of cool water; my brother's face, laughing. This style of communication must have been intriguing to my brother, for I would sometimes surreptitiously watch the two of them as they sat on the sofa in silence, my brother's face sometimes turning into a bright, beautiful smile that reminded me of my father, a smile sometimes followed (and this also reminded me of my father) by a burst of mirthful laughter. But all the while Skeery's face was the same inscrutable mask, her photosensitive skin pulsing with light.

I knew, of course, that what I was doing was wrong; after all, I had moved into their living situation—my brother's and Skeery's—and yet I could not help but feel as if it were I who had been imposed upon. One might forgive me my youth but there were plenty my own age who might have dealt with the situation with more grace.

"I'd like to meet her," Sim told me one afternoon as we lazed about upon one of the couches in the study hall. "She sounds fascinating."

"She's not fascinating," I told him in aggravation. "She's changed my brother's entire life. He can't even eat at home. He goes down the street to the café to take a shit because Skeery's too sensitive to the smell."

"Is it bad to change your habits for someone you love?" Sim asked me.

"She's not human," I said.

"Who is?"

"It's not a metaphor."

"It was meant as a joke," he said.

"Not funny."

"I'd still like to meet her," he told me.

"I don't think I'm ready for that," I said. "Not yet."

I wish now, of course, that I had brought Sim to meet Skeery. Perhaps something of his goodness, of his fairness, of his interest in situations and actions and people different from himself might well have taught me something of the grace I clearly lacked at that age. But I did not invite him to meet her, not then and not ever, for our relationship did not last for much longer after that conversation. I was utterly destroyed by the breakup at the time, although now, of course, it is easy enough to understand. I was so filled with anger and loss and loneliness that I must have felt, to Sim, like some black cloud ever-hovering around his head.

I had not even told my brother that I had been seeing Sim, not because I was trying to keep it secret but for reasons more petty. I simply wanted to keep it from him because I was angry at him due to Skeery's constant presence in our lives and, perhaps most of all, because I was lonely beyond measure, not only after Sim and I had broken up but before, a loneliness which was like a hollow space inside the whole of my body and which I did not think would ever be filled. So I had not told Victrola and yet I was angry when he did not display any real empathy for my renewed despair.

That it was Skeery who responded at last only conflated and complicated my ongoing sense of anger and betrayal and loss. Her communication was so quiet, so faint, that it seemed at first as if that trickle of images and words had come tumbling out of the background sounds of violins from my brother's screen.

You Hedgerow Quiet Sad Lost.

I looked up from where I sat in the dark corner of the room, staring at my screen. Skeery sat across from my brother at the table, her pale shift glowing blue from the thin tracks of her phosphorescent skin. She did not look at me, nor did my brother. I thought that he always heard her when she spoke to me, that she broadcast to both of us at the same time, but it appeared now that her communication had been directed to me alone.

I puzzled at the words, the flickering image of an ocean, an Earth ocean, and then silence again. And then another: *You Hedgerow Alone Negative.*

I sat looking at her but still she did not turn in my direction. I did not know what to do or what to say but at some point in the silence, Skeery rose and went to the small kitchen and heated a cup of water. My brother was looking up at her from his seat at the table now. They were clearly communicating and, although I could not hear them, my brother looked over at me, a look of sadness crossing his face.

"Stop talking about me like I'm not here," I said, my voice almost a shout.

"We're not," he said.

You Love Not Truth.

My brother shook his head. "She's right," he said. "She's making you a cup of tea. I asked her why."

"What did she say?"

"She said you broke up with your boyfriend."

I looked at him, incredulous, searching.

You Hedgerow Sim Gone Sad Home Place Now. An image first of Sim and then, just after, of a house in a field, chimney puffing with warm smoke, yellow lights in the windows.

I was on my feet now, my screen clattering to the floor. "Why do you know that? I didn't tell her that," I yelled into the room. Then I turned to her, to her mouthless, alien face. "I didn't tell you that!"

You Hedgerow Sad Tea.

Indeed she held a tray in her hand, the old-fashioned China teapot on its platter, the thin, gently cracked cup next to it, the set an heirloom which had been in our family for generation upon generation. My grandmother's. Her grandmother's before that. Why my brother had ended up with it I did not know.

This might have been the moment when I redeemed myself, when I sat and quieted my mind and listened to whatever it was Skeery had to say. That she was trying to help me was clear, but that she had taken from my mind a piece of information that I had not offered acted as a confirmation of all I had secretly suspected, all I had secretly feared.

And so, instead, I ran to the door and slipped outside into the dull cool of the air-conditioned night, my brother's receding voice calling my name until it was subsumed by the tangled and clangorous sounds of the Quay.

I stayed at a friend's apartment that night and for the next three nights to follow, but of course I could not stay there forever. My brother had messaged me and I had told him where I was staying—back in our old neighborhood not far from our family apartment—and his response had been a brief *OK* and nothing more. I did not know what I wanted him to do, but this response seemed utterly insufficient, and for many hours I secretly railed against him in my mind, against him, against Skeery, against my dead parents, against my lost home, against everything. My classes were tedium and my grades were slipping. I saw Sim sometimes at school, briefly, and he would smile and say hello and I would do the same and we would go our own ways, but the public mask was thin and my chest held a heart-shaped cup filled with ash.

I skipped school the following day and messaged my brother and asked if he would have a late breakfast with me at the waffle house near my campus. He agreed within seconds. I did not know if my brother had skipped his graduate seminar and I did not care to ask. I was angry with him still, but I also knew that my anger was petty and mean and under that pettiness was the fact that he was my only family and that I missed him terribly. If I was honest with myself, I knew I wanted the impossible: for the clock to draw backward over the cycles of day and night and day and night until my father was alive again and I was back in the old apartment and all was as it had been before.

I arrived at the waffle house before he did and was already seated when he slipped into the booth across from me. He looked, even at a glance, utterly exhausted, as if he had not slept for many nights. And yet it was he who asked me if I was okay.

I nodded. "She reads minds," I said.

His shoulders slumped. "She doesn't mean to," he told me. "But I hear you. I mean, I understand. It's a lot to get used to."

"I didn't tell her anything," I said. "Not one word. And she knew his name, Vic. His actual name. I didn't even tell you that."

"Why didn't you?" Victrola said. Our waffles had arrived and he was busily cutting his into bite-sized squares.

"I just hadn't gotten around to it," I told him. "That's all."

"All right," he said. "I'd like to know these things, though."

"That's just it. We can tell each other things if we want to. But she doesn't even ask. She just . . . it's just not right."

"It's hard for her, too," he said.

This last statement made me laugh, perhaps a bit too loudly, too dramatically.

"I don't mean it like that," my brother said. "I mean, it's hard for her not to listen. Human emotions are really loud for her. It would be like you or I trying not to listen to someone shouting at us over and over again."

"Boo-hoo," I said. "I'm sorry I'm making things difficult for her."

"Look," my brother said then. "I'm trying to be patient here."

"Are you?"

"Will you please shut the hell up for one second?" My brother's voice was loud now, louder than I had heard it in a very long time, loud enough, in fact, that the room around us quieted as if in response to his question. "It's not always about you, Hedge," he told me now. "You moved into our lives. Not the other way around."

"Believe me," I spat back, tears already streaming down my cheeks, "if I could live anywhere else I would."

"But you can't," he said. "So we have to make the best of it."

"I'm trying."

"Are you? Because it doesn't seem like you're trying at all."

I did not respond to this, although of course I knew it was the truth. I had been horrible and there was nothing I could do to change that fact. I felt as if some other me, some terrible demonic version of myself, had taken hold of the person I had once been, the person Sim had, I hoped, fallen in love with. But I had driven Sim away. What remained of me was a burning shell. A destroyer.

My brother may have called my friend's parents, because later that afternoon I received word that I would be staying with them for the remainder of that week. This gave me some sense of relief, although, as with everything during that period of my life, I was also conflicted about its meaning, interpreting it in ways that were likely far-flung from the reality. If it had been at my brother's request—and I did not ask him, nor my friend's parents, if this was true—I wondered what it might have meant. Did Victrola not want me in his apartment or was he simply offering me some time away from the presence of Skeery? Either way, I indeed took my friend up on her offer and returned to their much larger apartment with its familiar sounds of human voices running across the familiar smells of the cooking of human foodstuffs. I remember that I could not help but watch their mouths as they talked, as they ate, as they went about their evening routines. Once more I remembered Sim's mouth on my own, how our lips met, our tongues: an image that had come to me unbidden and which, even as I sat in that noisy apartment, filled me with longing and with loneliness.

By the time I returned to my brother's apartment at last I had made some decisions about Skeery. If we were to cohabitate, then we would need to get along, and I knew the main source of friction had come from me. In fact, were I truthful, I knew that Skeery had little to do with my discomfort. She was, in the end, only living her life and had, in fact, made room for me without any perceptible fuss whatsoever, this despite my sudden and unasked-for appearance in the cramped apartment she shared with my brother.

And yet, when I finally returned I knew immediately that something had changed. The very air inside was different and there was a sound, too, a kind of high humming that came from the wall where the little stove was located and which I realized, after a moment, was the refrigeration unit.

"Hey, Hedge," my brother said, coming out of the bedroom. He had apparently been sleeping, for his face and eyes were puffy.

"What's happening?" I said to him. And then, because the changes in the room were already dawning on me: "Where's Skeery?"

"She . . . uh . . . she moved out," he said, slowly, his voice stumbling over the syllables.

"Why?"

He shrugged, but his mouth was taut and he would not look at me.

"I'm sorry, Vic," I said.

"No, you're not," he said. "There's some food in the kitchen if you're hungry." Then he turned and disappeared into his room again. I wondered, as the door slid closed, if the banks of sunpanels remained within, their faces so black that it seemed a person could fall through them into whatever universe lay beyond.

Of course, my brother was right: I was not terribly sorry that Skeery was gone. I tried to maintain a sense of decorum around my brother, for he was clearly still wounded by her departure and still angry for my role in driving her away, but it was admittedly difficult. I felt free in the apartment now, free to talk and to watch whatever I wanted on my screens, and to generally lounge about as if I lived there, which, of course, I did. Victrola, on the other hand, seemed mired in shadow and even though a week and then another and yet another passed, that darkness did not depart, instead hovering about him from morning until night and, perversely, I felt my own moods lift as his descended, as if we were on opposite ends of a great seesaw.

He was quiet during those weeks, not silent but speaking only when necessary, doing his homework with great attention at the little table and occasionally retreating to the bedroom if I presented too much of a distraction with my constant chatter, my voice filling the emptiness that Skeery's absence and my brother's quietude had made suddenly apparent.

I knew he had cared for Skeery, of course, but I do not think I truly understood just how much her absence might affect him. Indeed, it had never occurred to me at all that she might leave him on my account, assuming that this was why she had moved out. (Again, I was young, and could hardly understand anything beyond myself, so I could only assume that her absence was directly related to me; the idea that she and my brother might have had a full emotional relationship with problems of its own did not occur to me at all.)

"You were right about one thing," he said to me one night, apropos of nothing at all.

"What's that?" I asked him.

"Kissing," he said.

"What about it?"

"I missed it."

I said nothing now, the heat of my shame flooding into my face.

"I couldn't even kiss her," he said. "I mean, how would that ever work? Long-term, I mean."

"I don't know," I said. "You said there was more to a relationship than kissing."

"Sure," he said, "but it's kind of fundamental, isn't it?"

"I guess so."

"You know, she could really feel," he said then. "The Blue can, I mean. It's how they are with humans. They can feel our emotions like waves. They don't feel each other like that, so for them, just feeling some human emotion—something positive, I mean—is like eating the best piece of chocolate cake ever."

"Chocolate cake?"

"Or whatever," he said, smiling a bit now at his own simile. "Love, for them—I mean, feeling human love—is the most amazing thing. It's like a drug."

There was a catch in his voice and I realized that my brother was on the verge of tears. "I didn't know emotions were so great for them," I said, hoping to steer him into some other, more clinical discussion.

"Only positive ones," he said quickly. "You know, like joy, love, happiness. Humor, even."

"Other stuff they don't sense?"

"Oh, I wish," he said. "Anger. Sadness. Frustration. Even something like irritation—all terrible. Skeery described it like smelling something dead or rotten. And they can't help but feel them, viscerally. Human emotions, I mean. The Blue can't turn that off. So, you know, she was like a sponge." For a long while he simply sat there at the table, staring at the darkened rectangle of the window, the sounds of the Quay muffled through the glass and the wall and the door.

I was crying then, crying as quietly as possible, but my brother, in his new raw grief, did not even seem to notice.

"I just missed kissing," he said absently, as if this explained anything at all. Then he took his screen from the table and disappeared once more into the bedroom he had once shared with his Blue.

The accident occurred a week later. I had taken a transport back from my school and had been peering at one of my screens with such intensity that I actually missed my stop—the first time I had ever done so—and when the transport stopped again I leapt off onto the platform without much consideration as to which station I had arrived at, noticing the sign for Loomtown only after the transport had whisked away. That I had never been in the Blue quadrant only speaks further of my own sheltered upbringing, so for a long while I simply stood upon the platform, watching the Blue pass in relative silence below me, the fluid motion hypnotic and beautiful, wondering if Skeery was somewhere down below and even hoping against all hope that I might find her figure amid the moving flow of pedestrians upon the sidewalk. And then, as if in response to my thought, I did indeed see one figure who reminded me strongly of Skeery, so strongly, in fact, that I nearly shouted her name. Of course, it was impossible that out of the population of the whole outpost I just happened to see the one person I had been thinking of, and yet the figure moved like Skeery moved and she was wearing the familiar pale white shift that she had worn each time I had seen her.

The decision I made was a split-second one, sprinting down the stairs and entering the flow of various pedestrians, mostly Blue with

occasional humans threading through their more sylphlike forms, following, as best I could, in the general direction in which Skeery—if it
was even her—had gone. Maybe I could reach her. Maybe I could apologize, tell her that she could come home—back to the apartment—that
my brother still loved her, that he wanted her back, that I could still fix
what I had broken, this one thing, this one beautiful thing I had, in my
own grief, burned to the ground.

Such were my thoughts as I passed down a sidewalk eerily quiet,
the various Blue around me not, of course, speaking aloud, so that the
only sounds were passing transports, my own clomping shoes against
the tarmac, the swish of clothing, and the occasional audible click of a
light turning on or off. It was into this quietude that I wanted to shout
Skeery's name, but I still did not know if it was really her, not until
the figure I pursued turned into an alley and I followed her, catching
full sight of her face just as she passed into an open doorway there,
realizing in that moment that it was actually her, that it was, indeed,
actually Skeery. This time I did call out, my voice a kind of echoing
boom against the now-closed door. I felt for the tickle of her consciousness against my own, but there was nothing. Quiet figures behind me
on the street. Larval-eyed.

On the door were characters in the language of the Blue. I did not
bother to look them up on my screen, instead pressing the sensor strip
to find the door unlocked and uncoded. The room I entered was a dark
cube striped with ribbons of glowing blue light that mimicked the skin
of the Blue, the gentle pulses moving in a direction that led me to a
narrow hall where the lights turned in rectangles around closed door-
ways. I listened for Skeery, my heart tight in my chest, not yet understanding where I was, or what the rooms and doors and the pulsing
light might indicate. Later I would wonder why I had failed to enter

the entry door's sign into my screen. I might have waited outside then, might have seen Skeery upon her exit, but instead had blundered into a place I should not have, this realization also coming much later, since, in the moment of my opening the door at the end of that hallway, all I could comprehend was the agony of my mistake.

It was much later, in the darkness of the many days and nights to come, that I reconstructed what I had seen and what had happened: The briefest sense of a large room. A dozen or more Blue both seated and standing in apparent communication. But already I was staggering back from the cold blazing sun of that alien world, my eyes stabbed through with an agony of immolation even through their clamped-closed lids, my arms up at my face. So bright, so unconscionably, interminably bright it could not be believed. And then a kind of wail which I understood, even in that moment, was coming from my own throat as I fell from the open door, fell backward, even as I could feel the press of alien consciousnesses entering my own, a garble of questions and images of sizzling flesh and flashes of light: *You Stranger Human Not Here*; *You Stranger Pain Pain Pain*; *You Stranger Help Danger Help Danger*. And then, from amid this cacophony of voices and images and my own agony and confusion, a familiar voice, shouting silently in my head: *You Hedgerow You Hedgerow Negative Negative Pain Help Help*, and then someone's hands on my arms, my body, lifting me from the tiles as if I were but a feather upon the air, my eyes still closed, red, streaming with pain, my voice rising in a kind of howl met, after a moment, by a faint shushing and the warmth of arms cradling my body, arms that had seemed like warm liquid enveloping me but now felt solid and strong and human. And then the voice: *It's all right now, Hedge.* It was a voice I recognized but did not recognize and I thought at first that it was somehow my brother's voice, but that was not quite right, for it was the voice of someone older, and as it continued to speak I felt myself melt into its softness even as the pain lessened and fell away. *You'll be all right, little Hedge. My little Hedgerow. Shhh. Shhh.* I could feel his lips against my eyes, my forehead, my cheeks, the warm scratch of his beard against my skin. And then I knew who it was, my father, my dear lost father, and even as I slipped into quiet unconsciousness the feeling that came over me in that moment was that I was safe and all would be well.

Of course, I never regained my sight. For a long while I did not understand what had happened when I had opened that door, what the light was, why it had blinded me, although this was, in the end, easy enough to explain. What confused me was the vision of my father that had come to me there as my optic nerves were burned to charcoal, for even in my memory it felt like he had been there with me not as a vision but in physical form, for I had felt his arms around me, felt his lips upon my boiling eyes, upon my forehead, upon my streaming cheeks. It had been him there, it must have been, it had to be, and yet the conscious part of my mind knew he had been dead for months.

My brother visited me often in the hospital. He was angry about Skeery, about the Blue in general, threatening all kinds of legal action, but that faded with time. After that, we mostly made small talk, although that quickly dwindled to long silences. There was, as it turned out, not much to talk about between us now. At some point during the long period of life skills training that followed my hospitalization, he brought some new woman, a human woman, to visit me. His new girlfriend. Now I cannot even recall her name.

As for Skeery and what happened to me, I had, by then, already figured out most of the story. I had happened upon the equivalent of a Blue restaurant, a social gathering under the simulated light of the Blue homeworld, a light brighter even than that which had been installed in the bedroom Skeery and my brother had once shared. It had blinded me and had burned my face, neck, and hands with enough severity to require skin grafts. It is perhaps a blessing that I cannot gaze at my own face, but the skin there is smooth and waxy to the touch, so I know it must not be a pleasant sight.

Given what happened to me, it may surprise you to learn that I have chosen to live with the Blue for most of the years since, not on the outpost upon which I had lived with my family but at a more distant base—much closer to the Blue's own homeworld—the designation of which will be meaningless to you, for its name is in the Blue's own language and consists of images rather than words. I can tell you that it is roughly equivalent to a cheetah leaping through a forest of bright green trees, although of course the animal in the Blue's language is no cheetah and the things that I call trees are hardly trees at all. Theirs is a poetic language and one which I have finally become adept at, although it has taken me all my life to reach mastery.

A few days ago, I was practicing that language with my tutor, Cern, much of which involved her teaching me how to listen to Blue conversation. I had reached a point where I could sense that someone in the area was communicating, but it always felt like a dull whispering from far away. I had been listening—or trying to listen—for a long while when something in the room's energy changed, a kind of musical wailing rising out of the darkness and then, from out of that wailing, something else, a familiar image: bright warmth, a great sun shimmering over a gently sloping hill covered in purple grass, the wailing slowing, fading, and the image holding for a long trembling moment before drifting away again.

You Hedgerow Hear Child, Cern said, the words matched by the image of a diminutive Blue.

You Cern Positive, I told him.

You Hedgerow Brightmemory, Cern said, the image of the purple hill returning in scattered outline, its vagueness meant to indicate, in Blue language, the general rather than the specific.

I had studied the Blue long enough to understand what Cern meant. What I had heard in that moment was a kind of lullaby, a common image meant to indicate that everything was still as it should be, that the world was warm and safe and kind. This was why the image had been of the Blue homeworld: that familiar purple hill and, to me, blindingly bright sun. Adults, too, sometimes used Brightmemory; in that context the use was unique to the recipient, a kind of living memory that the Blue could wrap around someone in distress or pain. For a child this might be a collective memory—the lullaby of security that was the Blue's homeworld—but for an adult, Brightmemory was often the gift of the recipient's very own best, safest memory, handed back to them in their time of need, filling their mind with security and pushing away pain and sadness and loneliness.

It was this thought, this overheard communication between a mother and child, that has brought Skeery back to my thoughts these years later and with it her own gift of Brightmemory in my time of greatest need, for of course it had been her lips against my eyes, against my forehead, against my cheeks, for although I did not know her at all, had never even tried, she had listened, unwillingly, to my own grief night after night in that tiny apartment and, when I needed it most, had clothed herself in that shape for my mind to find. Brightmemory. I can picture her outside the door in the pale shift that she always wore, luminous with her feeding as she lifted me and carried me away from that light and back into the shade of the human world. And then, through my shrieking, my blistering skin, my burned eyes, pushing away the pain with the brush of her impossible lips upon my face. And in that moment, sitting across from my tutor so many years later, the person I missed most of all was not my father or my brother but Skeery. I had never seen her again and learned much later that she had moved away from the outpost, much as I had, pushing farther into space, to the very edge of the frontier, for what purpose or reason I did not know, and while I had thought of her often in the years since the accident, there was something in the purple hill, the bright sun, the mother comforting a child in pain, that brought me back to those days after my father's death, when I lived in that little apartment in the Quay with my brother and Skeery. How I wanted to tell her that what she did for me had changed me as a person, not the blindness, although that had changed me as well, but understanding how it felt to be safe again, and right in that moment, at the age of fifteen, at the edge of adulthood when I could feel the whole of the world tipping into some unknown orbit, Skeery's kiss upon my burning eyes, Skeery's mouthless comfort upon my heart.

A RECKONING OF KISSES

Beth Ann Fennelly

—He placed his beer on the pool's lip, then pulled me into his. I'll wager that, on the scale of kiss-taste, a drag of Marlboro followed by a swig of Bud in a forbidden pool in the chlorinated dark still ranks pretty high.

—Through a chain-link. Soccer field. Drummer in a punk band.

—Curled around my firstborn's body, flesh-drunk, I kissed her chins and cheeks and tiny soft lips which parted, and for the briefest of moments we soul-kissed.

—I'd met the boy from the next town on my sixteenth birthday, in line at the DMV. He told me I was pretty and asked for my number. I'd never felt so grown up in my life. When he called, I said yes, so he picked me up and drove me to a lake with a boathouse. Once inside, he licked my face.

The next time he called I begged my sister to tell him I'd been sent to boarding school. She did, but charged me thirty minutes of back-scratching.

—Years before, my sister and I practiced on each other in a hotel bathroom. We also critiqued each other's "sexy walk." We never spoke of this again.

—After snowmobiling in Wisconsin. His lips were so chapped that they cracked mid-kiss and I swallowed his blood. I thought this should end up meaning more than it ended up meaning.

—Sitting on the fountain rim in Prague, I heard a commotion behind me. Before I could turn, something slicked the back of my neck—bird droppings?—and then the skinny back of a Romani ("Gypsies," I'd been warned by the Czechs, "all thieves") sprinted past, his hoot lingering after his boot soles flashed around the corner.

Was it a dare? An insult? Panicked flirtation? A distraction designed to remove my wallet from my bag? Here I sit, twice-my-life away, puckered, still responding to that kiss.

—The one with the girl. I kissed her not for her sake, or my own, but for the boys who were egging us on. Were I again presented with her soft lips, I'd do better.

—Strange that after all the lips, the censored kiss is the one I gave my daughter. Fourteen years ago I published a poem about it, which, the editor said, received some "interesting" feedback. Hate emails. All from women.

Recently, I found them. This time, they struck me as funny. Maybe, I thought—for so this world ripens us—maybe the women would, too.

—What's a kiss but two eels grappling in a cave of spit? Best not to overthink it.

—My grad school boyfriend had a mustache and beard. I didn't imagine I'd like them, but I did. I could kiss him for hours, the halo of scratchy hair making the central hot-soft even hot-softer.

But then came the month when we couldn't make rent, so he got a job delivering pizza, a spectacularly bad idea. Fayetteville's streets twisted around hills, and he had no sense of direction, so his pizzas were reliably late and cold. Tipping actually *was* just a city in China. Within three months he'd get rear-ended by a bozo without insurance. But I'm getting ahead of myself. What I wanted to tell you: drivers had to be clean-shaven. It was policy.

Before his first shift, he took a razor from its package. He entered the bathroom hirsute, and exited . . . wrong. I kissed him, and the kiss, too, was wrong. He slumped on the bed with his red, scraped jowls. "Wait a minute," I whispered, inspired, "I'll be right back." I took his razor and shaved "down there," shaved off every single hair. I thought it would be a turn-on, but I didn't feel sexy. Not at all. I looked like a child, like a Barbie. Now we were in it together, broke, depressed, slumped, razor-burned, and bald-jowled.

Reader, I married him.

—Today is our daughter's fifteenth birthday. These days, she and I rarely kiss.

———

—Maybe, at the end, there will be a reckoning of kisses. Maybe, along with good deeds, they tally our generosities of flesh. Maybe how we're judged is this: Were you a waste of breath? Maybe eternity feels like an endless kiss.

LATE-NIGHT SESSIONS WITH A BLACK LIBERAL PROGRESSIVE

Christopher Paul Wolfe

She was already in the bed when I came home. I could smell the incense burning from down the hall. It was coming from our room. Something called Black Gold. She'd picked it up from the African spot on the corner over the weekend along with two bottles of body oil, a bar of black soap, and an African medallion. I don't frequent this store often. From what I can see, when passing the storefront and its enthusiastic owner, the shit he sells just isn't the type of shit that I need. But she's always willing to give a motherfucker a chance.

I take off my coat and tie, shirt and pants, socks and shoes, and slide into the bed next to her, but I find that there's an extra head, sets of arms and legs, between us. They belong to my second-born, aka Number Two, aka the four-foot cock-block—I love him but, damn. I pick him up by his pieces and put them where they belong. When I return, I find her in the same position, lying on her side, her head turned away from me with a black silk scarf wrapped tight around her twisted wet locks.

She's making this steady sideways shift of her hips. If you don't know any better, you'd believe that she is either anxious or possibly aroused. But we've been married for six years, enough time to see two babies climb from her womb, enough time to have had more fights than either of us care to remember, over kids, money, infidelity—the typical shit that threatens a marriage as a going concern. Six years is enough time to know that she's just trying to put herself to sleep.

I slide across the bed and put my body up against her flannel pajamas. I kiss her behind her ear, down her neck, and along the ridge of her collarbone.

"You ain't getting none," she says, shrugging my lips off of her and turning farther into her side of the bed, farther away from me.

I lie there with a full view of the back of her covered head and those locks twined together like wet black ropes dangling down over her shoulders, saturating her pillow.

"So, it's like that?" I say.

"Please get your dick off my spine," she responds. "You're poking me."

"Baby, why are you acting like that?" I say, removing my erection, as she demanded, from the small of her back.

"Where have you been?" she asks.

"Hunting big game, baby. You know that. I've been trying to put food on the table."

"Well, I put the food on the table tonight," she says. "The food on the table, the kids in the tub, and now I'm putting *my ass to sleep*," she says, and keeps rocking her body. "And besides, you seem to have forgotten that I just got my teeth whitened."

"Whitened?"

She turns toward me and smiles so that I can see her pearly whites, which are as brilliant as Number Two's night-light, an observation that

I feel the need to verbalize in the moment. She responds by tossing her hips and backside against my body, a gesture she knows that I like, one that causes me to kiss her again, behind her ear, down her neck, and along the ridge of her collarbone. That shit is my signature move. It's kind of like the cheat code in *Contra*.

"Is there anything rolled up?" I ask.

"In the nightstand," she says.

I reach for the top drawer, open it, and rub my fingertips over a few items until they come upon a half-smoked blunt. I imagine she burned down what's missing in between cooking and bathing the kids.

"What took you so long to get home?" she says, slowly softening up.

"You know those white niggas, baby. They're not letting a brother leave until he's picked that corporate cotton." I light the joint, take a couple of pulls, and pass it to her. "One of those motherfuckers had the nerve to walk past my cube singing the theme song to *The Jeffersons*."

"Get the fuck out of here."

"Yeah."

"Did he know the lyrics?"

"Every. Fucking. Word."

"Did you sing it with him?" she says, laughing now. I mimic her for a minute before I burst into my own laugh, and then we laugh together. It's synchronized, almost harmonized. She passes the joint back to me.

"You think you're funny, huh?"

"That shit *is* funny," she says, as she tosses her hip and butt back into me.

Outside, a siren blares down our block. Neither one of us flinches, choosing to enjoy our subtle high and to take in the vibrant life of the city that surrounds us: pit bulls barking each other out, soft-soled police shoes chasing young brothers down our block—a pursuit that never stops—rats chewing our plastic trash cans, the sporadic discharge of a firearm through the night, a couple fighting, a couple fucking before they're back to fighting in the morning. Somehow, hearing it all never fails to remind us of us, lying here together at some other moment in time. The siren dies, and, if you listen close enough, silence comes to the forefront.

I grab my iPhone and put on some mood music. I start with something slow and old, borderline vintage, some Vandross, Guy, Sweat, even a song or two by that Chi-town nigga who shall not be named. Cats lost their way around the turn of the century, so I go no further than the nineties to avoid some new school, misguided crooner serenading my First Lady.

"You still trying, huh?" she says, hearing the first track come through the speakers. "You know, this is exactly why we have all of these damn kids."

"But I take care of them, though. And I can take care of *you* . . . if you let me." It's a risk to proceed like this, dropping phrases, knowing they've got too much room for interpretation, knowing that she might come back with something like:

"You take care of me? Negro, I work, got the same master's degree, but with a better GPA."

See what I mean?

"You know what I'm saying, baby." I make another run of the *Contra* code to get us back on track, assuming we were ever there. "I mean, let me *take care of you tonight.*"

I pass the *L* back to her. She takes two pulls and ashes it in an empty cup resting atop Frederick Douglass's Narrative on her nightstand. She's got his shit flagged with Post-it notes like she's working on a book report. At last, she turns toward me and places her hand against my ear, rubbing my upper lobe between her index finger and thumb, and says, "It depends."

"Depends? On what?" I ask.

"On if you can tell me how bad you want me," she says, and kisses my bottom lip in a way that sends my mind scrambling, grasping for the right answer. We've moved past the *Contra* code. What she wants, what she needs, is for me to stimulate her mental.

"I want you bad, baby," I say.

"I know you do. But how bad?" she says. "Tell me."

"I want you . . . I want you more than you want me to have Harden's beard and—"

"I never said that."

"I want you more than Ellis wants a pad and pen. I want you more than our pastor wants my offering."

"So, you're a rapper now?"

"For you, baby, I can get down like that," I say, and kiss her long and deep enough to taste the hemp on her tongue. "So, please, stop interrupting my flow, my rap."

"You're funny."

"I know, but listen to me when I tell you I want you more than a nineties nigga wanted his first Beamer, more than a dope fiend wants to get clean or another chance to feel the love from his fam, his team. I'm talking about that love like Martin had for this place despite its racist past. The love Coretta had for him despite his cheating ass."

"Yeah?"

"Yeah, baby."

She leans into me, and we kiss again. And then she looks at me and says to me, "You know I forgive you, baby."

"I know, baby."

"But I still want you to tell me more."

So I tell her, "I want you more than Hillary wanted Barack's soul. As bad as our people crave our true home. More than Kunta wanted to keep saying his name. More than Toby wanted to choke out master with his chains."

Suddenly her hand stops stroking my ear, and she begins to rub through my hair and down the side of my face. She kisses my lips and says, "Baby, you're going to be okay."

"I know, baby."

"Good. Now keep rapping to me."

So I keep rapping and flowing; in the background Luther keeps singing. I keep wanting and pleading until she knows that I need her to feel complete, until she slowly sheds her clothes, showing little concern for the slight chill in our bedroom. We kiss, and the way she sucks my lips is like a sobering manifesto. It's a wet and warm embrace that grounds my high, or quite possibly *is* my high. It tells me that there's no use for a *Contra* code. It says I know you better than you know yourself *on your best day*, so don't try to control me. Just love me.

So I did. And nine months later, I loved our Number Three.

AYLAN KURDI, AGE THREE

Matthew Komatsu

The aspect of the photo that pierces me most is his repose. Angled to sleep, face down and turned to the left on the wet sand of a Turkish shore. Hair black and wet with the Aegean. Red shirt, black shorts, feet sockless in his toddler's shoes.

So still.

I cannot help but imagine myself as his father, my son in his place. *It should have been me*, he said to the reporters. *Yes*, I think, *it should have been.*

We spotted a ripple of green beneath the torrent of a swollen creek. Easy to miss behind the constant surface flash of an Alaskan summer sun, it took us three legs in a trolling helicopter to spot the dead man's jacket waving in the current.

My teammate and I hoisted down from the helo to the trunk of pine tree that had fallen into the river. One of its stout branches had snagged the man's jacket. He was facedown, a foot beneath the surface, one arm extended upstream as the icy waters poured around him. Boils appeared and disappeared in the current, glacier-fed, whitewater upstream and down. It was not a place to fall.

So I held on to the tree and my comrade, while he wrestled with the snarled jacket twisted hopelessly around a branch too green to break. The current was strong, the waters frigid, and the man had worn chest-high waders that now acted like sea anchors filled with gallons of creek at peak flow. I mentally rehearsed what to do if I myself fell in, recalling my swift-water rescue training: *Feet downriver, paddle on your back towards shore, try not to die.*

In one photo, a Turkish policeman cradles the boy's body. Midstride up the beach, he looks away from the child held—no, *cradled*—away from his body with gloved hands. The Velcro straps upon the toddler's shoes, three of four secured, but the one: rent from its home upon the other half. Dangling, as if forgotten.

My son, now three, finds himself distracted amid haste. Too often, I react with anger at his inability to move with a sense of purpose, to complete a task as directed. Underpants donned inside out and backward, shirt pulled over his neck and arms dangling, he suddenly joins a world in which toy airplanes and cars have adventures and speak to each other. This, despite the clear and repeated orders and instructions, the adult world of deadlines and schedules. He is oblivious to my need for order.

Perhaps it was the same for the boy and his father. Perhaps this is what haunts Abdullah Kurdi to this day.

The body broke free of the branch and for a moment I thought we might lose it. But Aaron held on and was able to pull it out of the current and into the eddy downstream of the trunk we were balanced upon. We each took hold of what purchase his body provided: a bit of jacket, a belt, the pale, waterlogged flesh of his wrist. We strained against his weight until the creek relinquished him, belly-down on the tree, his waders emptying atop our feet.

We entered the hospital on the day my son was born, birth plan firmly in hand: Minimal interventions. No medication. All natural. My wife donned her gown, lay down on a gurney, and the admitting nurse took her vitals and attached a monitor to her stomach. She turned up the volume and we could hear the baby's heart, steady and strong. Then a contraction hit, and the *tum-tum* went silent. We asked if it was normal, but her face gave her away. No.

I took my wife's hand when the nurse disappeared, only to reappear with a team this time, all haste and whisper. The baby's heartbeat danced an erratic cadence across the screen, and they rushed us away, shouting, *Get a room ready*. Words like *distress* and *decels*.

In the room, another contraction struck my wife's uterus. She breathed, focused. All eyes fixated on the screen. The baby's heartbeat disappeared again and the room erupted in a flurry. A new monitor was attached to the finger of the obstetrician, who pushed it up the birth canal and onto the baby's head.

A pattern emerged: with every contraction, the baby's heart rate raced to rates impossibly high for me, a lifelong distance runner, to understand. And when the contraction ended, the beat dropped to the thrum of a zombie shuffle.

My wife endured, in position after primal position, self-conscious despite her pain and focus, of her tattered gown's indecency. And with each evolution, we held our breaths in the hope that this time would be different. But they grew worse, the oscillations between high and low dancing across the fetal heart rate monitor. The baby was hurting.

The obstetrician called it. *It's getting too scary*, she said.

An emergency cesarean. They cut him from the warm brine of his mother's womb. The sounds of suction, wet flesh, masked utterances whose meaning I could not comprehend as my wife's body shook with the force of their movements: all this amid the shine of cold metal and scentless air. I held her hand.

It's a boy, they said, holding him as for inspection. Head misshapen from the birth canal. Skin a gunky wet purple, eyes liquid black, he wailed at me from their hands.

But what they should have said was, *Mother, Father, here is your son.*

The gesture was futile, but necessary. I pressed two fingers to where his carotid artery once pulsed against the skin of his neck. There was nothing, had been nothing in the hours since his all-terrain vehicle overturned while it climbed the creek's bank, and dumped him to his fate.

Nothing to revive, no living lung into which I could press my breath, my lips upon his.

His ID was that of retired military: blue cardstock, black-and-white photo. Home of record identified as a bucolic suburbia outside Anchorage. Soon the phone would ring at that address. This father, this son; this husband and grandfather: *He returns to you as he came into this world.*

When I witness my son asleep, every defense against treacle falls away. It becomes impossible to see him as anything but perfect. I open his door nightly, applying odd pressure to preempt it scraping against the frame, and steal into the darkness. His space heater whirring, the air purifier humming: I kneel next to his big-boy bed and let my eyes adjust. When the curves of his face come into view, I can see how he sleeps with his hands pressed beneath his waist. Since the photo of Aylan, a great sadness often descends on me. I see, not a living child, but a boy—my boy—on that beach.

I match the curve of my lips to the bridge of his nose, a puzzle piece that has found its home. He does not stir, doesn't move. I press the kiss, hold my breath, and await the sound of his.

BAT VISION

John Mauk

Nedra stands in a cloud of dumpster stench, the moon hanging orange and low. She wonders what impulse made Justin show up. For an hour, he's been hunched in B2 with his back to the television. Why watch basketball or racing when you can watch your ex-girlfriend work? To boot, Gail's been on a rampage. Don't smoke if you've got tables. Stop leaving your butts on the ground. Don't fix your ponytail in the dining room. Don't yawn. Don't breathe. Curl up and die. But punch out first.

When she took the job at Lead Belly's two years ago, Nedra could hardly believe her luck. The pay was great. She started whittling down credit cards, offered help with utilities, which her mom accepted, and bought a candy-apple-red Grand Am with only twenty thousand miles. Each week, the money got designated for this and that. Now it's gone before it comes.

She takes the last drag, flings her butt at the ground, and twists her ankle like a washing machine. Despite the funk, she breathes deep, heads in, and passes the cooks calling each other names. Gimp. Buttmunch. At the swinging doors, she looks through the bubble, and sure enough, Justin is still there like white pudding on green leather, taking a whole booth for nothing but a Beer of the Month. And looky here. Gail is sidling up. They're having a nice chat. She's tossing her hair even though she's got nothing to toss. He's giving his lippy smile and sleepy eyes—a ruse, something loser doofuses master so they can ensnare women into hollow and orgasmless relationships.

In the office, she hangs her jacket. A wilted spinach leaf hugs the desk leg like flood debris. It's been there a while. Britney Spears pouts from the back wall. Someone recently gave her a yellow highlighter mustache, curlicues on both sides. None of it makes sense. Nothing in the world does—Britney next to the hand-washing guide, next to the Success photo with seven luxury cars, next to the coat rack, next to a giant crack in the paneling nobody will ever fix. How do people do it? Move from high school to something spectacular, something worthy of a poster or framed photo? Maybe you say yes to everything. Wear a girl's school uniform, glare over your ballooning boobs, and take whatever comes. Nedra's mother told her that—take whatever comes—right after her father packed up and zoomed to Florida.

Gail blasts through the swinging doors and says B2's sitting empty. Nedra considers saying—woman to woman—B2 isn't worth a full booth, won't order anything of substance, and won't tip for shit because that's how B2 operates. In fact, B2 doinked her pointlessly for two solid months until she woke up and realized one sweaty afternoon with his underwear half down and hers roaming by her feet that he didn't possess enough brainpower for kindness, romance, adventure, beauty, anything beyond a moany hump and follow-up sandwich. She doesn't have time to say all that because Gail is aimed for the cooks, already in mid-scold.

Nedra salutes Britney and punches the door. Past the pool table, she realizes something's off. The sound comes in waves, long collective vowels rising and trailing off. In the gap, someone cheers or screams. Nedra follows all eyes to a fluttering black thing, a maniac Kleenex flapping beneath the lights. People are putting placemats on their heads. A few bargoyles move to the floor and cover their beers with flattened hands. A few others swat with hats or menus. The cooks come out. Everyone's gawking, like on a snow day, those glorious seconds after the radio announcement comes and you're marveling because all bets are off, all wonder in full swing.

The jukebox volume goes down. Gail shows up by the server station, raises her arms, and pats the air. She tells everyone to sit tight. They're going to take care of it. No problem. Have some fun. Then she corrals servers and cooks to the back. Nedra follows, listens while Gail makes two points: One, keep it out of the kitchen. Two, ignore it. Heather asks how they're supposed to do both. Makayla says it'll get in someone's hair and then what? Phil says orders are probably up.

With a full tray, Nedra pauses to get her balance. The bat is now up beyond the lights on a tight clockwise orbit. She focuses, keeps her back straight and knees bent, tells herself bats aren't interested in people's hair—that it just wants out and far away. T2 hardly knows she's there but she does her thing—announcing each plate in careful rhythm: one medium rare burger with steak fries, cheeseburger medium rare with Swiss and fries, medium cheeseburger with cheddar, one barbecue chicken with extra sauce. She asks if everything looks okay, gets a nod.

She avoids B2, stops by B3, who wants battered shrooms and a round of kamikazes in honor of the bat. The jukebox is cranked again, louder than before. AC/DC. The big-haired women in T3 hoist beers and sing, "All night long!" A weekend regular, Jimmy Something, in T1 stands and plays air guitar. And then, somehow, for whatever reason, the bat is gone. Just like that. Some heads are still angled and scanning, but it's not in the rafters, by the skylight, or fluttering in a corner. It got tired or lucky, either settled somewhere or found a crack in the Lead Belly universe.

In the kitchen, she watches shrooms surface, twinkling and snapping. The new fry guy asks if they still have winged visitors. Nedra says maybe, maybe not. He hopes for more, a whole flock. Phil says it's called a colony, not a fucking flock. On her way out, she gets past the pool table, veers toward the station, and sees a dot by the Coors Light mirror. She stops, looks hard. The dot twitches. Or maybe it doesn't.

"Holy crap," Makayla says. "Is that it?"

"I think so."

"It's tiny."

"Get me one of those plastic containers, the ones for green onions."

"What are you thinking?"

"I don't know."

While Makayla goes, Nedra puts down the shroom basket and stares, trying to find a head, eyes, or tail. She moves in and squints. How does it work? Does the body have suckers?

Makayla's back. Nedra stays fixed on the dot, takes the container in both hands. She gets close, within inches, wonders if it's studying her approach, buckling its knees for a rocket-like fling. Before someone or something throws a wrench in the moment, she shoves. The plastic smacks the wall. Attention turns toward her. Voices feel close. She's got it, that waitress by the wall. The chick with the long ponytail. She pushes harder because maybe bats have crazy strength, can bash themselves free of anything. "I need the lid," she says.

"I didn't bring a lid."

"Get me a lid."

She keeps pressing and thinks of that old Beatles song her mom always sings. Nobody told me there'd be days like these. No shit, Ringo.

She hears Phil's voice. "Is that it? Do you have it?"

"I think so."

"That little brown spot?"

"Yes."

And then Gail's voice. "Is that it?"

"Yes," she says. "That is it."

"Here's the lid," Makayla says.

"How are you going to do it?"

"Those things carry rabies."

"Shut up, Makayla."

"Hey, it's a fact."

"Who's watching the grill?"

"Don't let it out."

"It'll be irritated now."

"Oh, man."

"Everyone shut up. Let her concentrate."

"This is cool."

"Let her concentrate."

She does what they're saying. She gets a grip on herself, concentrates. She scrapes the lid against the wall, sees her own ear and cheek in the Coors Light mirror, Gail's frizz behind her, Phil's mopey face, then a soup of bodies and colored light. This job wasn't supposed to be forever. It was a transition, a way to refresh before trying college again. Earn some money. Get your self-esteem back, her mom said. But self-esteem doesn't grow on trees, and it doesn't show up out of nowhere—Surprise! Here's your wherewithal!—especially when you live at home, sleep in your childhood bedroom, greet your mom's new boyfriend every morning in the kitchen, divert your eyes from his hairy gut, act nice but decline his eggs.

When the lid makes contact, she feels punky resistance, like Jell-O. She waits for a flutter or screech. There's neither. She scoops harder, imagines calling for a spatula. Shushes come from all directions, and then for no good reason the bat comes unstuck and plunks down like a turd. She presses the lid tight and brings it to eye level—a test for certainty. It weighs as much as a butterfly or cotton ball. The wings pry apart from its torso, and it rocks like it's crawling wounded and woozy from a rollover accident. Then the eyes open. Black beads. Some teacher or professor once said bats can see fine, no worse than a finch or sparrow, and if so, this little guy is witness to heavy stuff—rows of huge meaty faces blurred by plastic, a hundred eyeballs freakish and wide. He'll have nightmares or whatever bats have when they remember the worst. It blinks at her. Hello, Mr. Bat. Hello, Nedra. And if it weren't for the Rolling Stones song now pumping through the room, they'd whisper. She'd say everything will be okay. He'd say thank you. She'd apologize for everyone screaming like ninnies, swatting as if he were nothing but a bug. He'd ask, what is this place? She'd laugh and say, that's one hell of a good question. He'd laugh back because he'd understand. They'd commune, nod, agree on a million things. Then he'd ask, after taking a good look around, what's a nice girl like you doing in a rotten place like this? Well, Mr. Bat, it's a long and stupid story that starts with my dad hightailing a few years ago, leaving us with nothing but debt and sorrow, then my own failed attempt at college because I didn't understand rebellion and how it's a short-term deal with no reward. Mr. Bat would say something true and consoling, something about learning from your mistakes or rising up from the ashes, and if it weren't for the plastic between them and everyone watching, she'd offer him a kiss—not a romantic movie kiss but a tender human-meets-Muppet moment that makes kids and parents and bar managers with half a soul think, well, at least there's that. Her lips would meet his tiny puppy face and pug nose. His beady eyes would close and things would indeed be okay.

When applause comes, the bat flutters. She runs for the kitchen. Gail is yelling stuff, but Nedra keeps running. She shoulders the doors and curves around the prep table in one liquid motion. She gets past the dumpster and wades into the weedy field. Others are behind. Someone says to leave it—just leave it on the ground. She kneels, parts a swath of hard stems, and rests the container as flat as possible. She pops the lid on one side. The bat doesn't move. She can barely see, but he's still there, a silent glob. She pulls the lid toward her, then backs away. She waits, can hear shuffling, feel eyeballs on her back. Someone says to watch out. It'll fly into your hair. But it won't. He definitely won't. The two of them have an understanding. Anyway, you don't escape from something like that only to flap around in someone's hair. You take the opportunity. You launch yourself into open sky while the orange moon lights your way. You look down on the building, its flat tarry roof, the raucous cave beneath filled with strange creatures who'll sit and watch you suffer, who'll scream and holler and drink their drinks while your heart nearly explodes.

EIN KUSS IM KRIEG

Dave Essinger

How would you like that," the commandant asked, his face inclined to Franz's ear, "for those lips to be the last you know of this world?" His breath was heavy with the anise he took, that he said the ladies liked. He raised an eyebrow, waiting, as the two other soldiers from the morning's detail watched out of the corners of their eyes. He'd sworn he'd make a man out of Franz.

The courtyard had been a parade ground in better times, and its walls still sheltered against gusty spring winds, making what could have been a chill day temperate. They had brought the Belgian woman in to stand before the chipped wall, the spy, the dangerous beauty, and Franz thought she only looked frail, an embarrassment to the two hulking guards who held her arms.

Franz daydreamed in the soft sun and thought of Klara instead, and how fine it was to be married: they'd both confessed it a relief, to be settled at twenty and done with the courting and preening and making themselves attractive to others. He was lucky, for her, and for this home-front post, while so many of their former schoolmates were being conscripted for the Kaiser. He barely knew how to hold this new rifle.

His commandant went on, impatiently, "She poisoned them, you know. A deadly toxin, in the lipstick. Your last schmatzer, yes?" Immediately Franz wondered how this could be true, how any assassin could deliver a poisoned kiss without succumbing herself. And everyone knew the Field Marshal, seventy-two and morbidly obese, had collapsed in his potatoes at a state dinner, more the victim of a coronary than any seductress. Clearly, the administration had concocted a bald premise. Which by no means made the Belgian woman innocent: Franz had heard, in the newly gained territories, that no one could be trusted, not the civilians, even the women, that youths and servicemen who let their guard down were being murdered in bordellos and bars. Such ravenous hatred.

As if cued by Franz's thoughts, she straightened then and fixed the firing squad with a flirting look, an exaggerated moue from those allegedly infamous lips. The commandant asked which idiot had forgotten her blindfold, and a guard mumbled that she hadn't wanted one. Franz realized he would never be able to tell Klara about the spy, her painted lips, her contempt as she kissed the air at him, her obscene mugging. She was putting on a show, even now, a calculated act, and he wondered how many times her lips, if not poisoned then still venomous, had lied with a sigh, a little breath, *You kiss marvelously.* Franz remembered girls laughing and calling him clumsy, saying he kissed *like an ox, no, like some great monkey, no, haha, just like a trained circus bear!* At least he'd never been lied to, though, betrayed in that particular intimate way.

On his last leave home, Klara had apologized for the kriegsbrot, but had got hold of a little bratwurst, and dinner was good. When Franz pressed his lips to hers afterward, Klara received him and did not turn away. Klara had never told him he kissed well or badly. But now he wondered, how much pressure, should he move his lips more? Did his beard scratch her? She would never say it, even if he disgusted her, even if he'd neglected to wipe the sausage grease from his mouth. Suddenly anguished, he wondered how he could trust her with anything, if not that.

And Franz saw fully just what the spy had taken from him, was taking, even as she posed, mocking his misery. He had never been a vengeful person, when the injury was his own. But Klara did not deserve it, this shadow of his mistrust, that he did not see how he'd ever displace. His commandant barked, *Ready*, and then, *Aim*, then spoke so close his waxed mustache brushed Franz's ear, his breath cloyed with anise: "Fire, you fat bastard." And though they were supposed to sight for the heart, he let his aim drift higher, to those defiant pursed lips, as if to intercept that spiteful kiss still lingering unmet in the swirling indecisive spring air, before it could land.

THE KISSES WE NEVER GIVE

Kathryn Miles

We stood, a shifting cluster of humanity, pressed against the wooden railings of San Francisco's Pier 39. It was a temperate spring day, and the contrast between the warming sun and bitter ocean created little vortices of wind that ruffled T-shirts and sent all manner of hairstyles askew. It was also Mother's Day, a holiday that creates ripples of a different kind for a woman in a long-term relationship with a man and his two gorgeous boys. The boys were spending the day as they should have been, which is to say with their actual mother. The man, meanwhile, was stewing that work had once again taken me somewhere other than home. And so, on that awkward holiday, I was mostly whiling away the hours, first with wine and overpriced seafood, and then by playing tourist in a sea of couples and families.

Standing on that pier, we gaped as dozens of sea lions jockeyed for their own positions on similarly slatted floats. There was more than enough space to go around, and yet the massive animals tussled over the same small patch of real estate. As they did, we squealed and took lots of photos, singularly focused on the throng of mammals until one of us—a young woman in tight jeans and a brand-new engagement ring—noticed the two sea lions that weren't a part of the group.

"Oh, look," she said to her fiancé. "A baby."

At that, we all cast our gazes in the direction of the young woman's outstretched finger. There, on an otherwise empty float, a female hovered over her pup, nosing the top of its diminutive head and doing all the other things you'd expect a mother to do for her baby. We all watched and cooed until, one by one, it struck us:

Her pup was dead.

As this realization settled, it came first with collective silence, followed by awkward assertions about nature's will and lame jokes not even the tellers thought were funny. Some families moved on. Others stayed, bearing witness as the mother roared at any sea lion that came near. We flinched as she tugged her limp baby from one edge of the float to another, nudging its face and chest with her mouth in what, at the risk of anthropomorphism, can really only be called a series of frantic kisses. And as we continued to watch, I found myself hoping it would end: that she would realize the baby was dead and move on.

She didn't.

Eventually, I had to. I left for an interview not knowing when, if ever, this sea lion would leave her pup. And I carried the image of them both for the rest of that day and the next and the one after, when I returned home to the man and his two gorgeous boys. Months passed. As they did, our ripples became waves. The waves grew bigger. And then they broke, which is to say he broke, with a force that took my breath away.

"Like magma," our couples counselor tried to explain to me. And each time she did, she'd motion as if her chest had cracked wide and something uncontrollable now gushed out. That uncontrollable thing, she said, was a lifetime of pent-up rage. Whenever I asked her how to dam it—if such a thing could be mended—she'd shrug: "You have to wait it out," she'd say.

Instead I tried my own tugging and nudging, hoping something would soften—that this rupture would close, that trees and grass would begin to grow there again. Instead, it got worse. As it did, I found myself remembering that female sea lion, wondering if this was how she felt on that float.

We know just enough about other species to know that they do feel. Elephants display empathy by placing their trunks in one another's mouths. Magpies hold funerals for one another—gently pecking at a dead bird, then bringing it offerings. Bonobos make out. We don't know much about what mother sea lions do. They usually give birth and raise their pups in remote rookeries, which are hard to observe. What we do know is that it's not uncommon for a mother sea lion to tend to her dead pup for hours—or even a day or more. Whether this is an act of grief or an attempt to save the baby, scientists can't say. Nor do they understand when and why the mother eventually gives up. But when she does, she will abandon her pup where it rests and swim away, never looking back.

I didn't know how to do that. And so I spent that next season in a winter rental, thinking I would return home by spring. I went to our weekly counseling sessions, where the man railed about his anger and the counselor and I listened, dumbly nodding. I nudged harder, luring him to my new bed hoping I could fatigue his anger. He let himself be towed there. And in the resulting exhaustion, I grew hopeful.

But then I realized we sometimes don't know any more about our species than we do others.

On a cold February afternoon, and as swiftly as his magma had first erupted, the man left with his two gorgeous boys. There were no good-byes. One moment I was a family member; the next moment I was not. What came in its place was grief that crushed bone.

A farewell kiss can be the very sweetest. It can also slice right through you. But it's the ones left inside—the ones we never get to give—that often weigh the most. I cannot say why this is. Nor can I say why any animal—sea lion, human, or otherwise—remains with some-thing that has ceased to be. But I think maybe it's because we know on a molecular level that so few of our feelings die with a heartbeat, with a declaration, or even with a vanishing. And so we remain, hoping these feelings alone are strong enough to manifest a return.

ON WRITING THE INTIMATE

Brian Turner: Over the course of several email exchanges, I asked a handful of the writers included in this anthology to think about their own internal struggles and processes when they meditate and write about moments of intimacy—specifically when writing about the experience of *kissing*. Basically, I sent out a small questionnaire to each of them—a kind of Kinsey Report on literary kisses—and here are some of their responses . . .

1. **When attempting to write about an intimate moment, such as a profound and meaningful kiss, what is the single most challenging aspect of it for you?**

Benjamin Busch: Intensity. How do I join words to create electricity of the kind a kiss can have? I have to be dutiful to passion without concern for how I'll be seen in its light. In this case I just didn't think I was allowed any disguise, no protection from how vulnerable it made me. There's often a tendency to keep confession at a distance, to use retrospect instead of introspect as a way to hide. In a kiss, we forget to do the dishes, we drive off the road, our horizon warps and blurs. There are just the two people touching.

Pico Iyer: Intimacy is exactly what we're crying out for—because we're missing—in our super-accelerated, short-attention-span, distracted times. So I think a writer has a chance (you could almost call it a duty) to liberate the reader from the fast-forward roller coaster on which she's found herself and return her to that slower, more sensuous and spacious place she has inside her that has got overgrown or forgotten in our times.

It's hard, therefore, to get the reader to sit still long enough now to pay attention to a kiss, which is a perfect example of something that needs to be slow, absorbed, and heartfelt to be exciting; but that's exactly why we have to do it.

We live in the age of the blog, and the first-person narrative, which tempts us to forget that the personal is not necessarily the private, and that the felt is not always the deep. So in recording a kiss, I want to try to take the reader to that inner space where all thought of self is dissolved and we're ready to let go of everything we think we know and hope we can control.

Philip Metres: Of all the kisses that I could have written about, writing about a "shut-the-fuck-up" kiss to a competitor athlete on the basketball court was probably the least likely one to choose. It induced contradictory feelings of pride and shame, and that made writing about it intriguing to me. The most challenging aspect was laying bare those layers, some of which revealed my own human failings.

Major Jackson: With great effort, I tried to navigate the borders between the literalness of a kiss and its symbolism, but also, wanting to arrive at some insightful meaning. Whenever I see young people (and it's mostly always our youth) engaged in public acts of intimacy, I inevitably marvel at their boldness and feel the magnetic pull of intimacy.

2. **What are the pitfalls in writing intimate moments—and how do you suggest avoiding them?**

Nickole Brown: The question really is this: What *aren't* the pitfalls in writing intimate moments? The problem is with language—we simply don't have the adequate words to describe the complexities, especially when there is such a vast chasm between the way an act of love *looks* versus how it *feels*. A description that's too emotional will shorthand the experience with abstractions of love or desire, but one that's too literal will barrage with a tangle of lips and limbs, sort of as if one might try to describe the experience of a delicious meal by placing a tiny camera in the mouth. Make the mistake of the former, and your reader will dismiss the writing as sentimental; make the latter, and a whole undercurrent of feeling is often lost or, worse, will turn your reader off altogether. In reality, the joining of two people is a flood so complicated that it seems that literature might be the only form truly capable of not just handling the sensory details but the unpredictable fires hot with memories and other associations lit in the brain during intimacy.

Philip Metres: Writing about intimate moments is as fraught as any self-representation. Now more than ever, with the avatar-level self-fashioning of social media, it's easy to slip into creating a mere performance. Just as, when you were young, your bedroom moves were all imitations of what you'd seen on-screen, in films or videos. You're there but you're not there, not in the vulnerable place. You have to write past the performance and into the vulnerable place.

Sholeh Wolpé: I think when a piece of writing about an intimate moment does not work, it is because it lacks authenticity of experience. You can either translate an intimate experience, or you can re-create it. Translating a moment means: You are intellectually and factually accurate. You recount what happened. How you felt or what you saw. However, re-creating a moment for the reader requires marriage of fact *with* imagination. Did it feel cold? Then it *was* cold—even if it was eighty degrees and sunny. Was there a breeze? There was if you felt it.

3. **Among all of the kisses captured or explored in literature and art, is there one that you would point to as the North Star of them all?**

Camille T. Dungy: I don't know that I've ever thought about this question. It's a good question. I do love (in a tear-my-heart-out kind of way) the scene between David and Joey in James Baldwin's *Giovanni's Room*. The intensity of emotion Baldwin describes in that early scene shadows the entirety of that novel. But that turns out not to be a happy kiss. I wish I could bring my mind to settle on a happy kiss.

There is an amazing and beautifully intimate scene in the forthcoming novel *An American Marriage* by Tayari Jones. The kiss(es) in this particular scene I have in mind is one that I have been thinking about since I first read it. It's a kiss that I'm glad to know someone in the world has experienced. And it's a kiss that helped to make fictional characters feel to me like people who exist in this world.

Philip Metres: I love the curves of Auguste Rodin's *The Kiss*, that sense of twining and twinning. You can almost see the DNA helixing through them.

ROMEO: Sin from thy lips? O trespass sweetly urged! Give me my sin again.

Major Jackson: One of the ending lines in Dorianne Laux's poem "Kissing" states: "In a broken world they are / practicing this simple and singular act / to perfection."

4. **What does it mean for a reader to experience the joining of two worlds, as the depiction of a kiss suggests? That is, what can we, as readers, glean or experience in the literature of intimacy?**

Benjamin Busch: A moment of verse or prose that seeks to inspire human intimacy is an attempt at transference, a hope that another mind will be lit. That's the work of a messenger. I'm offering my dream to yours, hoping that your imagination and memory enter it, subvert it, subsume it and leave it behind. I want the reader to take my place. I want my words to be the reason that happens.

Sholeh Wolpé: Stanley Kunitz says, "Words are so erotic. They never tire of their coupling."

Camille T. Dungy: One of the things that is so tricky about describing kissing is that fine line between voyeurism (and its even less couth cousin, pornography) and what this project is working toward. When we write the kiss, when we read the kiss, we want to be welcomed into the wonder of the beauty of a world that is at the very center of the created creation. I once heard Jericho Brown say that he is a manifestation of the living God and so when someone touches him, when someone *loves* him, they are in touching God.

Those are my words for Jericho's, but the sentiment struck me to the core when I heard him speak it. One of the things that poetry can do is give sound to the inarticulate voice of creation. When we kiss, when we touch each other with love, we are touching the skin of creation. It's a gorgeous thing, this liminal space both great art and great intimacy bring us to live inside. It can be easily corrupted, and it is hard to watch someone else enter that space without wanting a fig leaf or some sort of mediation, because it can be so pure and so fundamentally perfect it practically sears. But if the writing is good, the reader can be present—not just as voyeur, but as participant.

Major Jackson: Intimacy abounds in the natural world; our carnality however, is conjoined with our ability to assign meaning, and it is our imagination and intelligence that I find the most erotic. More than appeasing our appetites for titillating details that may or may not arouse, pulling back the sheets so to speak on our most private moments gives us a fuller portrait of our humanity. Somehow, too, we are wrenched toward a greater enlightened space when we can do more than delight in the sensuousness of human contact. We are gifted a storehouse of images that models closeness and affection. Who couldn't use more of that in their lives?

5. **When writing about intimacy, is it crucial to have an element of the subversive included in the meditation?**

Nickole Brown: Many contemporary artists might consider an element of the subversive necessary to make a kiss effective in literature, but I don't agree. Shock and surprise and irony work at times to make such a sentimental and over-used topic new, but it's not the only way. For me, I prefer something more vulnerable—deep attention and a raw, muscular kind of seeing to defamiliarize those things we've all seen depicted too many times. I also think it's worth mentioning that saying a thing plainly and with your heart is worth the risk . . . Listen. We're human beings, all pretty much wired the same way. We yearn for companionship, for love, and need to be touched. You can subvert that all you want and it may get your readers' attention, but my guess is it won't stick, that they won't turn to that poem or passage again in a time of need. I'd rather encounter a weaker poem keenly felt than a clever one that leaves me cold.

Benjamin Busch: Intimacy is all subversion. Your sense of independence, your lone identity, is partially destroyed by that kind of invasion of privacy. Beyond that, in writing about it, readers take our words and construct their own version of our confessions. There should be a law . . .

6. **What makes a kiss profound? What makes it unforgettable?**

Major Jackson: A kiss is profound when it feels most singular—like a new planet being born.

Camille T. Dungy: I read/heard once that new atomic studies suggest that when you come in close contact with people in particular kinds of ways certain parts of your atomic matter leave the atoms that make up you and enter the atoms that make up them. But not really. The parts are still whole within themselves, they just stretch out and are also whole within the other. After hearing/reading this, I began to understand why some people I have loved still feel like they are a part of me, even when we have not been a part of each other's lives for a very long time.

Philip Metres: A kiss is a mere touch of the lips, but it's the electrical field of the body and mind electrified that make it memorable, that scores it into memory.

7. **Is there a connection between lyric suspension and an unforgettable kiss? That is, when the world sloughs away and time is upended, life swirling around a moment until all that seems to exist is the kiss and the singular moment of it—does this point us toward the eternal, the spiritual, the sublime?**

Benjamin Busch: We kiss each other mouth to mouth. It's a connection at the source of sound, where our language is spoken, where we eat and breathe. A deep kiss is an attempt to join another person at their most vital point. I don't know what gets at eternity, I'm not sure what counts as spiritual, but the sublime is at work in a kiss.

Major Jackson: Time is held at bay when one is kissing, properly. The demands and facts of our life seem to disappear and two people are their own purpose, far away from the banality of existence. Such transcendence is achieved by other means but every kiss is an echo of the very first human kiss, ancient and long-ago.

Sholeh Wolpé: I once kissed a man in an elevator at a writers' conference. The trip between the first and twelfth floor is continuing. My knees went limp and gave way. I would have collapsed had he not held me tight against himself, not relenting a second of that kiss which—if I close my eyes right now—is still happening, there in that elevator, moving up, never stopping.

CONTRIBUTORS

Kim Addonizio is the author of several books of prose and poetry, most recently *Mortal Trash*, a collection of poems (W. W. Norton, 2017) and a memoir, *Bukowski in a Sundress: Confessions from a Writing Life* (Penguin, 2016).

Kazim Ali's most recent books include *Sky Ward*, *Resident Alien*, and *Wind Instrument*. He teaches at Oberlin College. A new collection of essays, *Silver Road*, and a new collection of poems, *Inquisition*, will both be published in 2018.

J. Mae Barizo is the author of *The Cumulus Effect* (Four Way Books, 2015). A prizewinning poet, critic, and performer, recent work by her appears in *AGNI*, *Bookforum*, *Boston Review*, *Guernica*, and *Los Angeles Review of Books*. She is the recipient of fellowships and awards from Bennington College, the New School, the Jerome Foundation, and Poets House. Recent collaborative work includes projects with artists such as Salman Rushdie, Mark Morris, and the American String Quartet. She lives in New York City.

Laure-Anne Bosselaar is the author of *The Hour Between Dog and Wolf* (BOA Editions, 1997), *Small Gods of Grief* (BOA Editions, 2001), winner of the Isabella Gardner Prize; and of *A New Hunger* (Ausuable Press, 2007), selected as an ALA Notable Book. Her next book will be published by Four Way Books in early 2019. The editor of four anthologies and the recipient of a Pushcart Prize, she teaches at the Solstice Low Residency MFA at Pine Manor College.

Kurt Brown's (1944–2013) first book of poems, *Return of the Prodigals*, appeared from Four Way Books in 1999, and *More Things in Heaven and Earth* (also Four Way Books) in 2002. *Fables from the Ark*, which won the 2003 Custom Words Prize, was published by WordTech. *Future Ship* (Red Hen Press) came out in 2007, followed by *No Other Paradise* (also from Red Hen Press, 2010). Tiger Bark Press published *Time-Bound* in 2013, and *I've Come This Far to Say Hello: Poems Selected and New* in 2014.

Nickole Brown received her MFA from the Vermont College of Fine Arts, studied literature at Oxford University, was the editorial assistant for the late Hunter S. Thompson, and worked for ten years at Sarabande Books. Her first collection, *Sister*, was published in 2007 by Red Hen Press, and *Fanny Says* came out from BOA Editions in 2015. She was an assistant professor at the University of Arkansas at Little Rock for four years until she gave up her beloved time in the classroom in hope of writing full-time. Currently she is the editor of the Marie Alexander Series in Prose Poetry and lives with her wife, poet Jessica Jacobs, in Asheville, North Carolina.

Benjamin Busch is a writer, filmmaker, and illustrator. He served sixteen years as a Marine Corps infantry officer, deploying twice to Iraq. He's been a stonemason, sculptor, cartoonist, carpenter, and for three seasons he played Officer Colicchio on the HBO series *The Wire*. He's the author of the memoir *Dust to Dust* (Ecco, 2012) and his essays have arrived in *Harper's*, the *New York Times Magazine*, *River Styx*, *Michigan Quarterly Review*, and on NPR. His work has been featured in *Best American Travel Writing*, notable in *Best American Essays*, and awarded the James Dickey Prize for Poetry. His poems have appeared in the *North American Review*, *Prairie Schooner*, *Five Points*, *Epiphany*, and *Oberon*, among others. He teaches nonfiction in the MFA program at Sierra Nevada College, Lake Tahoe, and lives on a farm in Michigan.

Brian Castner is a nonfiction writer, former explosive ordnance disposal officer, and veteran of the Iraq War. He is the best-selling author of *All the Ways We Kill and Die* (Arcade, 2016), and the war memoir *The Long Walk* (Anchor, 2012), which was adapted into an opera and named an Amazon Best Book. His journalism and essays have appeared in the *New York Times*, *Wired*, *VICE*, the *Atlantic*, the *Boston Globe Magazine*, *River Teeth*, and on NPR. He is the co-editor of *The Road Ahead*, featuring short stories from veteran writers, and his newest book, *Disappointment River*, will be published by Doubleday in the spring of 2018.

Tina Chang is an American poet, teacher, and editor. In 2010, she was the first woman to be named Poet Laureate of Brooklyn. She is the author of the poetry collections *Half-Lit Houses* (Four Way Books, 2004) and *Of Gods & Strangers* (Four Way Books, 2011). She is co-editor of the anthology *Language for a New Century: Contemporary Poetry from the Middle East, Asia, and Beyond* (W. W. Norton, 2008). Her poems have been published in *American Poet*, *McSweeney's*, the *New York Times*, and *Ploughshares*, among others. She has received awards from the Academy of American Poets, the Barbara Deming Memorial Fund, the Ludwig Vogelstein Foundation, the New York Foundation for the Arts, *Poets & Writers*, and the Van Lier Foundation, among others. She teaches poetry at Sarah Lawrence College and was also a member of the international writing faculty at the City University of Hong Kong, the first low-residency MFA program to be established in Asia.

Steven Church is the author, most recently, of the nonfiction books *Ultrasonic: Essays* (Lavender Ink, 2014), *One with The Tiger: Sublime and Violent Encounters Between Humans and Animals* (Soft Skull Press, 2016), and *I'm Just Getting to the Disturbing Part: On Work, Fear, and Fatherhood* (Outpost19, 2018). He edited the anthology *The Spirit of Disruption: Landmark Essays from The Normal School* (Outpost19, 2018) and is both a founding editor and nonfiction editor for *The Normal School: A Literary Magazine*. He coordinates the MFA program at Fresno State University.

Adam Dalva is a graduate of NYU's MFA program, where he was a Veterans Writing Workshop Fellow. He was an associate fellow at the Atlantic Center for the Arts and a resident at the Vermont Studio Center. Adam teaches creative writing at Rutgers University. His work has been published by *The Millions*, *Tin House*, *Guernica*, the *Guardian*, and others. He is also a dealer of French eighteenth century antiques.

Mark Doty is the author of nine books of poetry, including *Deep Lane* (W. W. Norton, 2016); *Fire to Fire: New and Selected Poems* (Harper Perennial, 2009), which won the 2008 National Book Award; and *My Alexandria* (University of Illinois Press, 1993), winner of the *Los Angeles Times* Book Prize, the National Book Critics Circle Award, and the T. S. Eliot Prize in the UK. He is also the author of three memoirs: the *New York Times*-bestselling *Dog Years* (HarperCollins, 2007), *Firebird* (Harper Perennial, 2000), and *Heaven's Coast* (Harper Perennial, 1996), as well as a book about craft and criticism, *The Art of Description: World into Word* (Graywolf, 2010). Doty has received two NEA fellowships, Guggenheim and Rockefeller Foundation fellowships, a Lila Wallace/Readers Digest Award, and the Witter Byner Prize.

Andre Dubus III's books include the *New York Times* bestsellers *House of Sand and Fog* (W. W. Norton, 1999), *The Garden of Last Days* (W. W. Norton, 2008), and his memoir, *Townie* (W. W. Norton, 2011). His most recent book, *Dirty Love* (W. W. Norton, 2013), was a *New York Times* Notable Book selection, a *New York Times* Editors' Choice, and a *Kirkus* Starred Best Book of 2013. His new novel, *Gone So Long*, is forthcoming. Mr. Dubus has been a finalist for the National Book Award, and has been awarded a Guggenheim Fellowship, the National Magazine Award for Fiction, two Pushcart Prizes, and is a recipient of an American Academy of Arts and Letters Award in Literature. His books are published in over twenty-five languages, and he teaches full-time at the University of Massachusetts Lowell. He lives in Massachusetts with his wife, Fontaine, a modern dancer, and their three children.

Camille T. Dungy is the author of four books, most recently *Trophic Cascade* (Wesleyan University Press, 2017). Her debut collection of personal essays is *Guidebook to Relative Strangers: Journeys into Race, Motherhood, and History* (W. W. Norton, 2017). She edited *Black Nature: Four Centuries of African American Nature Poetry* (University of Georgia Press, 2009) and co-edited the *From the Fishouse* poetry anthology (Persea, 2009). Her honors include an American Book Award, two Northern California Book Awards, a California Book Award silver medal, and fellowships from the Sustainable Arts Foundation and the National Endowment for the Arts. Dungy is a professor in the English Department at Colorado State University.

Martín Espada was born in Brooklyn, New York, in 1957. His latest collection of poems is called *Vivas to Those Who Have Failed* (W. W. Norton, 2016). Other books of poems include *The Trouble Ball* (W. W. Norton, 2011), *The Republic of Poetry* (W. W. Norton, 2006), *Alabanza* (W. W. Norton, 2003), *A Mayan Astronomer in Hell's Kitchen* (W. W. Norton, 2000), *Imagine the Angels of Bread* (W. W. Norton, 1996), and *City of Coughing and Dead Radiators* (W. W. Norton, 1993). His honors include the Shelley Memorial Award, the Robert Creeley Award, the National Hispanic Cultural Center Literary Award, the PEN/Revson Fellowship, and a Guggenheim Fellowship. *The Republic of Poetry* was a finalist for the Pulitzer Prize. His book of essays, *Zapata's Disciple*, was banned in Tucson as part of the Mexican-American Studies Program outlawed by the state of Arizona, and has been issued in a new edition by Northwestern University Press. A former tenant lawyer, Espada is a professor of English at the University of Massachusetts Amherst.

Dave Essinger's recent fiction, creative nonfiction, and poetry appears in various literary journals, and his new novel about ultrarunning, *Running Out* (2017), is available from Main Street Rag. He received his MFA from the School of the Art Institute of Chicago, and is a fiction reader for *Slice* magazine and general editor of the AWP Intro Journals Project. He currently teaches creative writing and edits the literary magazine *Slippery Elm* at the University of Findlay in northwest Ohio.

Siobhan Fallon is the author of *You Know When the Men Are Gone* (G. P. Putnam's Sons, 2012), which won the 2012 Pen Center USA Literary Award in

Fiction, a 2012 Indies Choice Honor Award, the 2012 Texas Institute of Letters Award, and was listed as a Best Book of 2011 by the *San Francisco Chronicle*, the Los Angeles Public Library, and Janet Maslin of the *New York Times*. Theatrical productions of her stories have been staged in California, Colorado, Texas, and France. More of Fallon's work has appeared in *Women's Day*, *Good Housekeeping*, *New Letters*, *Publishers Weekly*, *Huffington Post*, *Washington Post Magazine*, and *Military Spouse* magazine. Her first novel, *The Confusion of Languages* (G. P. Putnam's Sons, 2017), is about two American women navigating the Middle East during the Arab Spring. Siobhan currently lives with her family in Abu Dhabi, United Arab Emirates.

Beth Ann Fennelly directs the MFA program at the University of Mississippi, where she was named Outstanding Teacher of the Year. She's won grants and awards from the NEA, United States Artists, a Fulbright Fellowship to Brazil, and a Pushcart Prize. Fennelly has published three books of poetry and one of nonfiction, all with W. W. Norton, and a novel co-authored with her husband, Tom Franklin. She's currently finishing a collection of micro-memoirs.

Nick Flynn has worked as a ship's captain, an electrician, and as a caseworker with homeless adults. His most recent book is *My Feelings* (Graywolf, 2015). A new collection of poems, *I Will Destroy You*, is forthcoming from Graywolf.

Kimiko Hahn is the author of nine collections of poetry, including *Brain Fever* and *Toxic Flora*. Both of these were triggered by rarefied fields of science in much the same way that previous work was triggered by Asian-American identity, women's issues, necrophilia, entomology, premature burial, black lung disease, and so on. A passionate advocate of chapbooks, Hahn's latest is *Resplendent Slug* (Ghost Bird Press, 2016). She teaches in the MFA Program in Creative Writing and Literary Translation at Queens College, City University of New York.

Cameron Dezen Hammon is a writer and musician whose work has appeared in or is forthcoming from *The Rumpus*, *Ecotone*, the *Houston Chron-*

icle, The Butter, The Literary Review, Brevity's Nonfiction Blog, Columbia Poetry Review, The Brooklyn Review, Literary Orphans, and elsewhere. Her essay "Infirmary Music" was named a notable in *Best American Essays 2017*. She is cofounder of The Slant reading series, host of *The Ish* podcast, and teaches creative writing to fifth graders through Writers in the Schools. Cameron's music has been featured on Houston Public Media KUHF, Houston Pacifica Radio KPFT, as well as the PBS television programs *Skyline Sessions* and *Oxford Sounds*. She earned her MFA from Seattle Pacific University and is at work on a memoir about religious and romantic obsessions.

Terrance Hayes is the author of *Lighthead* (Penguin, 2010), *Wind in a Box* (Penguin, 2006), *Hip Logic* (Penguin, 2002), and *Muscular Music* (Tia Chucha, 1999). *How To Be Drawn* (Penguin, 2015) is his most recent collection of poems.

Pico Iyer is the author of two novels and ten works of nonfiction, including such bestsellers as *Video Night in Kathmandu* (Knopf, 1988), *The Lady and the Monk* (Knopf, 1991), *The Open Road* (Knopf, 2008), and *The Art of Stillness* (TED Books, 2014). He has also written introductions to more than sixty other books, as well as liner notes for Leonard Cohen, a screenplay for Miramax, and words for a piece by a New Zealand chamber orchestra. Based in Nara, Japan, since 1992, he contributes regularly to the *New York Times*, *Harper's*, the *New York Review of Books*, and many others, and has seen his books translated into twenty-three languages. He currently serves as Distinguished Presidential Fellow at Chapman University.

Major Jackson is the author of four collections of poetry, including *Roll Deep* (W. W. Norton, 2015), which won the 2016 Vermont Book Award and was hailed in the *New York Times Book Review* as "a remixed odyssey." His other volumes include *Holding Company* (W. W. Norton, 2010), *Hoops* (W. W. Norton, 2006), and *Leaving Saturn* (University of Georgia, 2002), which won the Cave Canem Poetry Prize and was a finalist for a National Book Critics Circle Award. Jackson has published poems and essays in the *American Poetry Review, Callaloo, The New Yorker*, the *Paris Review, Plough-*

shares, Poetry, Tin House, and in several volumes of *The Best American Poetry.*
He is the recipient of a Whiting Award, a Guggenheim Fellowship, a Pushcart Prize, and a National Endowment for the Arts Fellowship, among other
honors. He serves as the poetry editor of the *Harvard Review.*

Lacy M. Johnson is a Houston-based professor, activist, and is author of the
memoir *The Other Side* (Tin House, 2014). For its frank and fearless confron-
tation of the epidemic of violence against women, *The Other Side* was named
a finalist for the National Book Critics Circle Award in Autobiography, and
was awarded the Dayton Literary Peace Prize, an Edgar Award in Best Fact
Crime, and the CLMP Firecracker Award in Nonfiction; it was a Barnes and
Noble Discover Great New Writer Selection for 2014, and was named one
of the best books of 2014 by *Kirkus, Library Journal,* and the *Houston Chronicle.* She is also the author of *Trespasses: A Memoir* (University of Iowa Press,
2012). Her third book, *The Reckonings,* is forthcoming from Scribner in 2018.
She teaches creative nonfiction in the low-residency MFA program at Sierra
Nevada College and at Rice University.

Christian Kiefer is the author of the novels *The Infinite Tides* (Bloomsbury,
2013) and *The Animals* (Liveright, 2015), and the novella *One Day Soon Time
Will Have No Place Left to Hide* (Nouvella, 2016). He is the recipient of a Pushcart Prize for his short fiction and is a contributing editor at *Zyzzyva* and
a fiction reader for *VQR.* Kiefer has a long second career in music, under
the auspices of which he has collaborated with members of Smog, Sun Kil
Moon, Wilco, Low, and the Band. He holds a Ph.D. in American literature
from the University of California at Davis and is the director of the low-
residency MFA at Ashland University. He lives in the foothills of the Sierra
Nevada northeast of Sacramento, California, with his wife and family.

Matthew Komatsu is a writer based in Anchorage, Alaska. A veteran of the
wars in Iraq and Afghanistan, he is a graduate of the University of Alaska
with an MFA in nonfiction. His work has appeared online and in print in
the *New York Times; War, Literature & the Arts; Brevity; The Normal School,* and

other fine literary establishments. As he is still in uniform, he is obliged to remind the reader that his words do not represent official policy or position.

Ilyse Kusnetz (1966–2016), poet, essayist, and journalist, is the author of *Small Hours* (Truman State University Press, 2014), winner of the T. S. Eliot Prize for Poetry, and *The Gravity of Falling*. Her next book, *Angel Bones*, is forthcoming from Alice James Books in 2019. Her work has appeared in *The New Yorker, Orion, Rattle, Guernica Daily, Islands Magazine*, and *Crab Orchard Review*, among others, as well as in anthologies, including *The Room and the World; The Book of Scented Things; Devouring the Green: Fear of a Transhuman Planet*; and *Monstrous Verse: Angels, Demons, Vampires, Ghosts, and Fabulous Beasts*. She also guest-edited Scottish poetry features for *Poetry International* and the *Atlanta Review*. Kusnetz taught at Valencia College in Orlando, Florida, where she lived with her husband, Brian Turner. Ilyse and Brian recently collaborated on a poetic text called "Vox Humana," which premiered with the Buffalo Symphony Orchestra.

Ada Limón is the author of four books of poetry, including *Bright Dead Things* (Milkweed Editions, 2015), which was named a finalist for the National Book Award in Poetry, a finalist for the National Book Critics Circle Award, a finalist for the 2017 Kingsley Tufts Award, and one of the Top Ten Poetry Books of the Year by the *New York Times*. Her other books include *Lucky Wreck* (Autumn House Press, 2006), *This Big Fake World* (Pearl Editions, 2006), and *Sharks in the Rivers* (Milkweed Editions, 2010).

Rebecca Makkai is the Chicago-based author of the novels *The Borrower* (Penguin, 2012) and *The Hundred-Year House* (Penguin, 2015), and the collection *Music for Wartime* (Penguin, 2016)—six stories from which have appeared in *The Best American Short Stories* and *The Best American Nonrequired Reading*. The recipient of a 2014 NEA Fellowship, Makkai has taught at the *Tin House* Summer Workshop and the Iowa Writers' Workshop, and is currently on the faculty of the MFA programs at Sierra Nevada College and Northwestern University.

John Mauk grew up on the Ohio flatland. He has a Ph.D. in English from Bowling Green State University. His stories have appeared in a range of fine magazines such as *Arts & Letters*, *New Millennium Writings,* and *Salamander.* He has also contributed essays to online magazines including *Writer's Digest, Beatrice.com, Three Guys One Book, The Portland Book Review,* and *Rumpus.* His first short collection, *The Rest of Us* (Michigan Writers Cooperative Press, 2012), won the Michigan Writers Cooperative Press chapbook contest. His first full collection, *Field Notes for the Earthbound* (2014), is available from Black Lawrence Press. He currently teaches at Miami University and lives whenever possible in Traverse City, Michigan.

Christopher Merrill has published six collections of poetry, including *Watch Fire* (White Pine Press, 1995), for which he received the Lavan Younger Poets Award from the Academy of American Poets; many edited volumes and translations; and six books of nonfiction, among them *Only the Nails Remain: Scenes from the Balkan Wars* (Rowman & Littlefield, 1999); *Things of the Hidden God: Journey to the Holy Mountain* (Random House, 2005); *The Tree of the Doves: Ceremony, Expedition, War* (Milkweed Editions, 2011); and *Self-Portrait with Dogwood* (Trinity University Press, 2017). His writings have been translated into nearly forty languages; his journalism appears widely; and his honors include a Chevalier from the French government in the Order of Arts and Letters. As director of the International Writing Program at the University of Iowa, Merrill has conducted cultural diplomacy missions to more than fifty countries. He serves on the U.S. National Commission for UNESCO, and in April 2012 President Obama appointed him to the National Council on the Humanities.

Philip Metres is the author of *Pictures at an Exhibition* (University of Akron Press, 2016), *Sand Opera* (Alice James Books, 2015), *I Burned at the Feast: Selected Poems of Arseny Tarkovsky* (Cleveland State University Poetry Center, 2015), *A Concordance of Leaves* (Diode Editions, 2013), *To See the Earth* (Cleveland State University Poetry Center, 2008), and others. His work has garnered a Lannan Fellowship, two NEAs, six Ohio Arts Council Grants, the Hunt Prize for

Excellence in Journalism, Arts & Letters, the Beatrice Hawley Award, two Arab American Book Awards, the Watson Fellowship, the Creative Workforce Fellowship, the Cleveland Arts Prize, and a PEN/Heim Translation Fund grant. He is a professor of English and the director of the Peace, Justice, and Human Rights Program at John Carroll University in Cleveland.

Kathryn Miles is the author of four books, including *Quakeland: On the Road to America's Next Devastating Earthquake* (Dutton, 2017). Her essays and articles have appeared in dozens of publications, including *The Best American Essays*, the *Boston Globe*, *Ecotone*, the *New York Times*, *Outside*, *Popular Mechanics*, and *Time*. She currently serves as writer-in-residence for Green Mountain College.

Dinty W. Moore is author of *The Story Cure: A Book Doctor's Pain-Free Guide to Finishing Your Novel or Memoir* (Ten Speed Press, 2017), the memoir *Between Panic & Desire* (Bison Books, 2010), and many other books. He has published essays and stories in the *Southern Review*, the *Georgia Review*, *Harper's*, the *New York Times Sunday Magazine*, *Arts & Letters*, *The Normal School*, and elsewhere. A professor of nonfiction writing at Ohio University, Moore lives in Athens, Ohio, where he grows heirloom tomatoes and edible dandelions.

Honor Moore's most recent book is *The Bishop's Daughter* (W. W. Norton, 2009), a memoir, a finalist for the National Book Critic's Circle Award and a *Los Angeles Times* Favorite Book of the Year. Her most recent collection of poems is *Red Shoes* (W. W. Norton, 2006). Her work has appeared in *The New Yorker*, the *Paris Review*, *American Scholar*, *Salmagundi*, the *New Republic*, *Freeman's*, and many other journals and anthologies. For the Library of America, she edited *Amy Lowell: Selected Poems* (2004) and *Poems from the Women's Movement* (2009), an Oprah summer readings pick which is featured in the documentary about American feminism, *She's Beautiful When She's Angry* (2014). She has been poet-in-residence at Wesleyan and the University of Richmond, visiting professor at the Columbia School of the Arts, and three times the Visiting Distinguished Writer in the Nonfiction Writing Program at the University of Iowa. Moore currently lives and writes in New York, where she is on the graduate writing faculty of the New School.

Aimee Nezhukumatathil is the author of four collections of poems, most recently *Oceanic* (Copper Canyon Press, 2018). Her collection of lyric nature essays is forthcoming from Milkweed. Honors include a Pushcart Prize and a fellowship from the National Endowment for the Arts. She is poetry editor of *Orion* magazine and a professor of English in the MFA program at the University of Mississippi.

Bich Minh Nguyen, who also goes by Beth, is the author of three books: the memoir *Stealing Buddha's Dinner* (Penguin, 2008), which received the PEN/ Jerard Fund Award; the novel *Short Girls* (Penguin, 2010), which received an American Book Award; and most recently the novel *Pioneer Girl* (Penguin, 2015). Her work has been widely anthologized and featured in numerous university and community reading programs. She is a professor in the MFA in Writing Program at the University of San Francisco.

Téa Obreht's debut novel, *The Tiger's Wife* (Random House), won the 2011 Orange Prize for Fiction, and was a 2011 National Book Award finalist and a *New York Times* bestseller. Her work has been anthologized in *The Best American Short Stories* and *The Best American Nonrequired Reading*, and has appeared in *The New Yorker*, the *Atlantic*, *Harper's*, *Vogue*, *Esquire*, and *Zoetrope: All-Story*. She was a National Book Foundation 5 Under 35 honoree, and was named by *The New Yorker* as one of the twenty best American fiction writers under forty. She lives in New York, teaches at Hunter College, and is married to Dan Sheehan, with whom she often revives the debate outlined in their essay in this book.

Kristen Radtke is the author of the graphic nonfiction book *Imagine Wanting Only This* (Pantheon, 2017). She is the art director and New York editor of *The Believer* magazine. She lives in Brooklyn.

Suzanne Roberts is the author of the award-winning memoir *Almost Somewhere* (Bison Books, 2012), as well as four collections of poetry. Her work has been published in *Creative Nonfiction*, *Brevity*, and *National Geographic Traveler*, among others. She holds a doctorate in literature and the environment from the University of Nevada, Reno, and teaches for the low-residency MFA programs at Sierra Nevada College Tahoe and Chatham University. She lives in South Lake Tahoe.

Roxana Robinson's most recent novel, *Sparta* (Picador, 2014), was named one of the Ten Best Books of the Year by the BBC, and was short-listed for the Dublin IMPAC Award. It won the James Webb Award from the USMCHF and the Maine PWA for Fiction. She is the author of four other other novels, *Cost* (Sarah Crichton, 2008), *Sweetwater* (Random House, 2007), *This Is My Daughter* (Random House, 1988), and *Summer Light* (Viking, 1988), as well as three story collections and a biography of Georgia O'Keeffe. Four of these books were *New York Times* Notable Books. Robinson's work has appeared in *The New Yorker*, the *Atlantic*, *Harper's*, and *The Best American Short Stories*, as well as the *New York Times*, *Harper's*, *Tin House*, the *Wall Street Journal*, the *Washington Post*, and elsewhere. Robinson was named a Literary Lion by the New York Public Library, and has received fellowships from the NEA, the MacDowell Colony, and the Guggenheim Foundation. She teaches in the MFA program at Hunter College. She lives in New York City.

Schafer John c is a writer, actor, and fisherman. Born and raised on the north side of Chicago, where he was shot, he was a member of the Latino Chicago Theater Company and earned a degree in sociology from Illinois State University . . . after playing basketball for five different colleges. As an actor, he's appeared in a number of films and on *The Drew Carey Show*, *Dharma & Greg*, and *SeaQuest DSV*. He's played everyone from a jealous boyfriend, to a brooding sculptor, to a horny vampire. His screenplays for *Bruised Orange* and *The Unconcerned* have been produced and his short stories have appeared in *Amor Fati*, the *Writer's Compass*, *Short Story* magazine, and *Guernica*. He's fished in Brazil, Vietnam, the Baja, the Yucatán, and . . . northern Michigan. He lives in Virginia, where has just finished *Transcendental Blues*, a novel in three parts, and is at work on more. He can't stop.

Dan Sheehan is an Irish fiction writer, journalist, and editor. His writing has appeared in the *Irish Times*, the *Los Angeles Review of Books*, *Guernica*, *TriQuarterly*, *Words Without Borders*, *Electric Literature*, *Literary Hub*, and numerous other publications. He lives in New York, where he is the Book Marks editor for *Literary Hub* and a contributing editor at *Guernica* magazine, and was a recipient of the 2016 Center for Fiction Emerging Writers Fellowship. His debut novel, *Restless Souls*, will be published in 2018 by Weidenfeld & Nicolson (UK) & Ig Publishing (U.S.).

Tom Sleigh's many books include *Station Zed* (Graywolf, 2015); *Army Cats* (Graywolf, 2017), winner of the John Updike Award from the American Academy of Arts and Letters; and *Space Walk* (Mariner, 2008), which received the Kingsley Tufts Award. In addition, *Far Side of the Earth* (Houghton Mifflin Harcourt, 2003) won an Academy Award from the American Academy of Arts and Letters, *The Dreamhouse* (University of Chicago Press, 1999) was a finalist for the *Los Angeles Times* Book Prize, and *The Chain* (University of Chicago Press, 1999) was a finalist for the Lenore Marshall Prize. He's also received the PSA's Shelley Prize, a Guggenheim, two NEAs, and many other awards. His poems appear in *The New Yorker, Poetry*, and many other magazines. In February 2018, Graywolf is publishing *The Land Between Two Rivers: Poetry in an Age of Refugees*, and a book of poems, *House of Fact, House of Ruin*. He is a Distinguished Professor at Hunter College and has worked as a journalist in the Middle East and Africa.

Patricia Smith is the author of eight books of poetry, including *Incendiary Art* (TriQuarterly, 2017); *Shoulda Been Jimi Savannah* (Coffee House, 2013), winner of the Lenore Marshall Prize from the Academy of American Poets; *Blood Dazzler* (Coffee House, 2013), a National Book Award finalist; and *Gotta Go, Gotta Flow* (CityFiles, 2015), with photographer Michael Abramson. Her work has appeared in *Poetry*, the *Paris Review*, the *Washington Post*, the *New York Times, Tin House* and in *The Best American Poetry, The Best American Essays*, and *The Best American Mystery Stories*. She is a Guggenheim fellow, a National Endowment for the Arts grant recipient, and a two-time winner of the Pushcart Prize. Smith is a professor at the College of Staten Island and in the MFA program at Sierra Nevada College.

Ira Sukrungruang is the author of *The Melting Season* (Burlesque, 2016), *Southside Buddhist* (University of Tampa Press, 2014), *In Thailand It Is Night* (University of Tampa Press, 2013), and *Talk Thai: The Adventures of Buddhist Boy* (University of Missouri Press, 2010). He teaches in the MFA program at the University of South Florida and edits the online journal *Sweet: A Literary Confection*.

Christopher Paul Wolfe, a North Carolina native, graduated from West Point in 2000 and spent six years serving as a U.S. Army officer. Wolfe holds an MBA from Duke University and is currently completing his MFA at Columbia University, where he also has served as a teaching fellow and led the Veterans Writing Workshop at Columbia University. His writing has appeared in *Penthouse*, *Guernica*, *Veoir*, and, more recently, in *BOMB* and the veterans anthology *The Road Ahead: Fiction from the Forever War*. Wolfe resides in Bed-Stuy, Brooklyn, with his wife and three children, and is working on a novel.

Sholeh Wolpé is an Iranian-born poet, writer, and public speaker, and is a recipient of a 2014 PEN/Heim Translation Grant, 2013 Midwest Book Award, and the 2010 Lois Roth Persian Translation Prize. Wolpé's literary work includes four collections of poetry, two plays, three books of translations, and three anthologies. About Wolpé's latest collection of poems, *Keeping Time with Blue Hyacinths* (University of Arkansas Press, 2013), *Shelf Awareness* magazine writes, "A gifted Iranian-American poet beautifully explores love and the loss of love, beauty and war and the ghosts of the past." Wolpé's modern translation of *The Conference of the Birds* by the twelfth-century Iranian mystic poet Attar (W. W. Norton, 2017) has been hailed by Reza Aslan as a translation that "is sure to be as timeless as the masterpiece itself." She has lived in the UK and Trinidad and is presently based in Los Angeles.

EVERLASTING KISSES

A book on kissing wouldn't be complete without a page filled with kisses for all who made this great assembly of meditations on kissing possible . . .

To you, who hold this book in your hands: *Thank you*. I hope it surprises and delights you. May all of your kisses be profoundly meaningful, forged in joy.

I'm grateful for the generosity of spirit shown by all of the writers who contributed to this anthology—as they have not only helped to create a wonderful book, but they have made the following donations possible . . . In honor of my late wife's wishes to support the work of inventor Boyan Slat and his efforts to remove plastic from the world's oceans, 50 percent of the proceeds from this book are being donated in her name to the organization The Ocean Cleanup (https://www.theoceancleanup.com). The remaining 50 percent will support the editorial internship program at *Guernica* magazine.

This project began online at *Guernica* magazine with the creation of a bimonthly series called "The Kiss." As one of the cofounders and former editor-in-chief of the magazine, Michael Archer supported and encouraged the series, teaming me up with the truly phenomenal Ed Winstead. Ed and I have worked together ever since to bring *Guernica*'s readers the most breath-taking literary kisses possible, rain or shine. I'm thankful to the publisher and director at *Guernica*, Katherine Rowland, for all that she has done to see this project through.

I'm grateful to all at W. W. Norton—especially my editor, Alane Salierno Mason. Her great patience and belief in this project have remained steadfast and true, and her guidance has, at every step, aided me in the pursuit of a profound and necessary book, one worthy of a reader's eye and ear. I send kisses and thanks to all at W. W. Norton—for believing that this world needs the sexy and the spiritual, the profane, the bewildered, the beautifully incandescent and transcendent, the many layers of intimacy and connection that kisses bring.

Many thanks go to my agent, Samar Hammam at Rocking Chair Books, who kindly donated her time on this project. I've been blessed by our many years of friendship and our conversations on art, life, and all that matters most. My hope is that we will shepherd many more books toward the rare high shelf, and that our conversations will deepen and brighten as we go.

To Alison Granucci and to all at Blue Flower Arts: Thank you for creating the journeys that have opened up a wider world for me and have given me the gift of friendships, year after year. *Much love, always.*

I'm indebted to the polymath genius and artistic vision of Benjamin Busch. He's not only written a beautiful meditation for this anthology, but he also served as an early eye for many of the essays and stories that appear in this book. The original artworks he created for some of the early essays that appeared online are superb and set the bar for the field. His friendship is a compass fixed on all that is luminous.

Special thanks to Tony Barnstone, Stacey Lynn Brown, Kim Buchheit, Skip Buhler, Matt Cashion, Russell Conrad, Sarah Cossaboon, Roel Daamen, Nathalie Handal, Patrick Hicks, Didi Jackson, Major Jackson, Lois P. Jones, T. R. Hummer, Christian Kiefer, Krista and Henk, Benjamin and Serena Kramer, Jared Silvia, Bill Tuell, and to all in the Retro Legion. To each of you, and to all of my friends and family and teachers: *Thank you for the light and love you bring to this world.*

Most of all, I would like to thank Ilyse Kusnetz. This book would not have been possible without her unconditional love and encouragement, as well as her keen and unerring editorial eye. Behind the scenes and from the very beginning, she pored over each meditative essay for the series at *Guernica*; her insights and edits are at work throughout this anthology, sentence by sentence, word by word.

Ilyse—

I will meet you at the great door when my time has come—
as you have traveled, so brave and beautiful and brilliant,
into the unknown ahead of us . . .

My love, if there is a vault of kisses within the human frame
housing my soul, then you are the key to unlocking them.

All of my kisses are for you.